EMBRACE

— YOUR —

AUTHENTIC

Songwriter

How & Why to Play Your Own Tune

Beth Kille

Cover design by Erik Kjelland, Noon Thirty Design. Back cover photo by Marsha Mood.

To contact Beth Kille directly visit www.bethkille.com

ISBN 979-8-35093-713-8

To Mom and Dad

Contents

Part Two............................61

FOREWORD

As a high school senior, my English teacher invited us to write stories about whatever we wanted. This was the seed that would later blossom into my songwriting. Though I didn't know that then, I did know it was the only learning activity I did in four years of high school that felt joyful. Like other teenagers, I was experiencing new friendships, budding romances, and increasingly difficult academics. At times, I also witnessed racism and friends' overuse of alcohol and drugs. As is likely true for many young people, there was a lot to navigate. Through writing "fictional" stories about what was going on in my world, I was able to process and find my way through these experiences. As a result, my burden was lighter. In college, I dove deep into The Indigo Girls' and Peter Gabriel's music. In their songs, I felt a sense of belonging. Growing up, I had listened to pop radio and its many breakup songs. I had also learned to play classical piano pieces. However, Peter, Amy, and Emily's deeply psychological and philosophical lyrics gave me a space where I uniquely recognized myself (I thought, "Oh, other people think about these things too?!" and "Maybe I'm not such a weirdo after all."). It was likely while listening to the song "Come Talk to Me" or "Watershed," that I first thought, "If I ever write a song that feels this true and moving, my life will have been worthwhile."

Years later, after I'd been working as a touring singer-songwriter, I was invited to teach songwriting at various places like GRAMMY Camp, Berklee College of Music, Interlochen, and songwriting retreats across the country. At first, I didn't know if other people would use songwriting the way I had (as a place to process relationships, grieve losses, celebrate victories, etc.). What I found is that many approached songwriting in this way. Even when people came to a workshop primarily to have fun, they often used the songwriting opportunity to work through a challenge or loss. Through these experiences, I realized that songwriting has unique features that can help one get to know oneself better and that it can be a potent healing practice in one's journey towards wholeness.

Enter Beth Kille, author of this book! Perhaps more than any other songwriter I know, Beth is all about songwriting as a journey toward wholeness! Through reading this book, you will come to love her as a person, value her tips and tools, and discover how songwriting can possibly be this for you too!

Beth Kille is an open, loving, kind, extremely silly soul who relates to others easily and teaches in a non-hierarchical way. You know Beth is leading because she's standing on stage talking into the mic. However, you never feel like she's "above" you. I first met Beth through Girls Rock Camp Madison, where, for several years, I watched her lead songwriting workshops for groups of up to 40 campers. In this role, she is self-effacing, funny, and, most importantly, she takes away the notion that songwriting needs to be a) difficult or b) something you need innate skill to do.

Beth breaks songwriting down into small pieces and uses fun writing prompts (such as giving campers random objects to write about). She also has boundless amounts of energy to inspire and support. If you doubt yourself, Beth's enthusiasm will carry you until the point you don't doubt yourself any longer.

She's 100% dedicated to letting people know that their voices, points of view, and experiences matter! To Beth, it's a given that everyone is worthy of being heard loudly and listened to closely.

Beth engages with songwriting holistically. As a physical therapist and as someone who studied psychology, Beth loves helping people maximize their potential and lead balanced lives. She knows that just as we are healthier when we eat healthy food or exercise, we are also healthier when we create in ways that light us up. Authentic songwriting is one of those ways. When we write our truth, we stay current with ourselves, express emotions, and connect with our body, mind, and spirit.

Over the years, cultural narratives about successful bands have often included drama, drugs, and the harming of self. In Beth's world (and mine), this is an old paradigm that no longer needs to apply. Authentic songwriting is not only a fun way to take good "emotional care" of oneself, it also fosters positive relationships and builds resilient communities. Every summer, I see campers who are afraid to talk to each other until they find something they want to write a song about (like being the first woman president or not being judged for their appearance) and they are off and running!

When people express themselves honestly through song, they are vulnerable and powerful at the same time. They are vulnerable for sharing their truth and point of view. They are powerful for being brave enough to write and share it. When people write songs together, they share, integrate, and make something out of their authentic parts. This creates a strong bond between people who now give each other the benefit of the doubt, which can be a rare thing in the world these days. Beth embodies this way of thinking and being and shares it with her students and community!

This book you have in your hands is a treasure that will continue to give to you for as many times as you read it and do the exercises. Beth is a gentle and loving guide. Consider this book your chance to learn about songwriting and yourself. Consider it an opportunity to love yourself more fully!

– Anne Heaton

PREFACE

Hello, dear reader. You may be wondering what prompted me to write this book. First off, I thought, "I have many things to share about songwriting." I am an avid reader of books on songwriting and music business as well as genres ranging from fiction to self-help. Books have helped me, and I like to help people, so I decided to write a book that others might find helpful. That's deductive reasoning from Philosophy 101, baby.

There are a few things I want you to know before you dive into this book. One is that I'm a goofball and I tend to get animated when I talk. Also, I get super-duper excited when people embark upon a creative journey. So, if you want to capture my tone, please read my words with a healthy dose of gesticulation, a side of snideness, and a heaping dollop of unconditional love directed at your inner songwriter. I am like that slightly embarrassing mom in the bleachers, wildly cheering you on, no matter where you are in the pack. Or you can picture me as that happy-scrappy dog who greets you enthusiastically at the door, listens with eagerness to every brilliant word you speak, and then hides your sneakers just for fun. Oh, and I will bite anyone who tries to hurt you. Just sayin'. There's no room for creative bullies in my house.

I've written this book for anyone interested in exploring songwriting. If you've never written a song before but have the desire, great! If you've already written some tunes and want to expand your skills, fabulous! There are three parts to this book. Part 1 is a philosophical dive into why music exists and what it means to you and your listeners. In part 2 we'll explore specific lyric writing and basic musical techniques to apply to your tunes. Part 3 is intended to personalize all you've gathered throughout the book, so you can confidently and authentically step forward into your life as a songwriter.

I'm going to ask you to do the work. Embracing your authentic songwriter requires discipline. I've included assignments at the end of each chapter to guide you. I encourage you to read this book near a device that allows you to look up lyrics and listen to the song examples I use. If you play guitar or piano, you'll need your instrument within arm's reach. If you're a novice guitarist, have a chord chart handy so you can look up the chords I reference. Your songwriting muscles will strengthen with practice.

It might be tempting to skip parts 1 and 3 so you can focus solely on the nuts and bolts of songwriting, but I'd urge you to reconsider. I've attended and taught songwriting workshops for many years and have found that there is a lot of effort put into teaching people *how* to write. For example, there are tons of resources to help you with lyric writing. And there are certainly books you can buy on music theory. And, of course, we can all find teachers willing to show us how to use our instrument(s) of choice (guitar, piano, drums, voice, etc.). But funny enough, I have never attended a workshop on *why* we write. (Shout out to Nancy Moran, who does a fabulous workshop on finding your "why" for being in the music business.) Why is it that we don't give as much thought to *why* we write? We all have our own reasons; I hope to connect you with yours.

In part 2, I share a bit on "how" to write. I put the word "how" in quotes because I firmly believe what I tell people at my workshops all the time: the number one rule in songwriting is that there are no rules in songwriting. I prefer to think of the tidbits in this book as *tools* you can use like a hammer you pull out of your toolbox when you need to drive in a nail. I have seen some incredible performing songwriters look at me like, "What in the world are you talking about?" when I start to mumble about music theory in a cowriting session. And I can think of other amazing performing songwriters who have never taken a songwriting class or read a book on writing songs. They just have a gift and have figured out a lot of things by trial and error (e.g., "Hey, people clap really loud when I play this song . . . I guess this one is good!").

You might have a gift too. But maybe every once in a while you get stuck. That is when you should open your toolbox, pull out something you learned, and apply it, so you can get past the barrier. Maybe all your songs are starting to sound the same and you need to bust out of a rut. Applying some newly learned tricks might spark your creativity. But never, ever, ever do I want you to think, "Oh, the book says I should write using this formula, so I can't do *that.*" Ahhhhhhhhh!!!!!!!!!! NO! No and just . . . *no.* That is not what any of this information is for. Yes, I just ended a sentence with a preposition. Why? Because I'm a songwriter, darn it, and I don't believe in rules.

The right half of our brain controls the left half of our body and the left half of our brain controls the right side. The left and right hemispheres of our brains are responsible for different executive functions (although there is some overlap and a lot of variability from person to person). Left-handed people are often referred to as "right-brain dominant" and right-handed people are considered "left-brain dominant." This isn't a hard-and-fast neurological rule, but right-brain dominance often causes lefties to lean more toward creative, big picture thinking, while right-handed people tend to be more logical and structured.

I am somewhat ambidextrous. With my left hand, I write and throw a frisbee (a critically important life skill). With my right hand, I do most other things: sports, playing guitar, sewing, and using scissors. Then there are activities that confuse me, so I switch hands, like playing ping pong, putting on eye makeup, and using a fork. I often feel that there is literally a battle going on between the hemispheres of my brain. The right half is always trying to dream big, follow butterflies through the field, and write snippets of songs that flitter around with the butterflies, never to land. Then the left half of my brain will kick in and say, "Settle down, Beth, and finish the task at hand. Organize your kitchen, write the second verse to that song, and stop chasing butterflies."

I think this is quite handy, though (pun intended). If your habit is to identify more strongly with one of the hemispheres and never fully engage the other, it might make your songwriting life more difficult. I hope to give you the tools to engage both halves of your brain, along with your whole heart.

Full disclosure: I do not have a formal degree in music and I am not a hit songwriter, at least not by Billboard's standards. And while what I have to share certainly could propel you to write songs that make you a lot of money, that isn't what matters to me. This is a book to give you the tools so that you will become the best songwriter you can be.

I tattooed the word "Inspire" on my left forearm for my 40th birthday. It's my personal mission to connect people with their creative spirits so they can express themselves and share all their beauty with the world. I believe every song is a gift. I hope you find inspiration in these pages and share your gifts. Thank you for joining me on this journey.

PART ONE

In part 1 of this book, we're *not* going to get into the nitty gritty of songwriting. Nope. We're doing a deep dive into *you*. We're building your songwriter foundation. We're going to examine why people listen to music; the role of a healthy body, mind, and spirit in creativity; your personal musical origins; and your unique purpose for writing.

CHAPTER 1

WHY PEOPLE LISTEN TO MUSIC

Seek first to understand,
then to be understood.
—Steven R. Covey, *The 7 Habits of*
Highly Effective People

True listening is a skill. Admittedly, I often find myself using only a fraction of my attention to listen to the person sitting across from me. Often my mind starts thinking about my response instead of hearing my partner through to the end. Sometimes I'm simply preparing to add to their story, or maybe I'm gearing up to argue my point. Or worse, I'm just waiting to change the subject back to me, myself, and I, because I really *am* fascinating, you know (insert seductive hair-flip here). But when I work to truly shift my focus to the speaker before me, quiet my brain's internal chatter, and clear my judgments, something amazing happens: I learn. And my heart and mind are expanded in unexpected ways.

Have you ever asked yourself why anyone would want to listen to your music? And, backing up even further, why do people want to listen to music at all? If you're like me, you write because you have something to *say*. But how can we come to understand why someone might want to *listen*? Understanding this will deepen our connection to our creativity and help us grasp how our songs may serve a larger purpose.

Human Connection

From a Darwinian stance, it may appear that art offers no advantages when it comes to avoiding an untimely demise. It's not like you could stop a charging rhino with a perfectly-executed I, IV, V chord progression and a pithy bridge. But perhaps there are evolutionary advantages to the human connections created by art. Music strengthens and deepens our interpersonal bonds and can make us healthier beings.

It's hard to deny that listening to music creates connections. Whether it be the crowd syncing up with the rhythm section of a funk band, or the swell of a symphony's strings taking your breath away, or your heart skipping a beat when someone else's song perfectly expresses the way you feel—music is a way for humanity to intertwine. Isn't it incredible that a musician can impact us physically without ever laying a hand on our bodies? It's almost as if there are invisible threads between us, stitching us into one human fabric. That has a certain survival purpose, doesn't it? Existing as an interconnected pack seems like a classic example of safety in numbers.

Knowing that we're not alone in the world absolutely has a positive psychological impact. Psychotherapist and mindfulness and meditation teacher Tara Brach states, "Our most fundamental sense of well-being is derived from the conscious experience of belonging. Relatedness is essential to survival."[1] Have you ever felt like you were wrong or crazy for thinking or feeling a certain way? I know I have. But the truth is that there are a finite number of emotions humans can feel, yet sometimes we think we're the only ones who have ever felt "that way." Then someone comes along and sings a song that makes us realize they've been there too. Wow! That is a relief, isn't it?

If you're not familiar with them, look up the lyrics to Radiohead's song "Creep." I've seen this song performed numerous times and it never fails to amaze me the diverse group of audience members singing along. I think everyone can relate to the feeling of being the outsider, the weirdo, the one who doesn't fit in. Every time I hear this song, I think, "Thank goodness we're all together in our aloneness!"

The funny thing is, songs don't even have to have words to create a human connection. Whether it's some kind of hard-wired neural circuitry, or simply a product of our upbringing, or a combination of both nature and nurture, musical sounds have the capacity to elicit strong emotions in our listeners.

Playing with Our Emotions

Robert Jourdain, author of *Music, The Brain, And Ecstasy: How Music Captures Our Imagination*, argues that our emotional reactions are a product of our "anticipations" being either met or unmet.[2] When we expect something to happen and it does, or it exceeds our expectations, this is satisfying and elicits positive emotions. For instance, say you show up to a work meeting and unexpectedly learn you're getting a raise. Woot!! But when we anticipate something and it doesn't happen, then we feel a longing for that sense of fulfillment. For example, we go to the store to buy milk and learn that the dairy truck never came. Now we feel a longing for that milk we can't have on our cereal.

The way we structure our songs, both rhythmically and

melodically, can set up our listeners for repeated disappointments and satisfactions. It may sound strange that listeners want to be "disappointed," but delayed gratification is an incredibly strong psychological tool. If music is entirely predictable, it's boring. If there is no predictability at all, it feels chaotic. I believe the best composers are those who learn to walk the line between predictability and chaos. They make their listeners feel a bit of longing by creating tension with the music, melody and/or lyrics, and then they deliver well-timed catharses.

I'll share more about how to do this in part 2. For now, just know that there are tricks you can play with your chord progressions, melodies, and lyrics that can create tension and then release it. Understanding that listeners *want* you to tug on their emotions (whether they know it or not) can be a powerful tool in your composition.

Emotional Expression and Modulation

Speaking of emotions, I believe art helps us connect with the full range of emotions that make us human. If you have any doubt that music and emotion are connected, consider this: Have you ever watched a movie that has no soundtrack? Probably not. Why is that? Music supervisors are the professionals tasked with placing audio over visual media. A good music supervisor carefully selects the music to heighten the emotional impact of the action and dialogue. When the tone of the music matches the emotional tone of the movie scene, we are completely enraptured. Musical mismatch can evoke feelings of irony, like a comically disastrous scene with happy music. Music modulates the viewer's emotional experience (and undoubtedly boosts engagement).

Even in the absence of moving pictures, listening to music can be cathartic. I'm the type of person who spontaneously cries when I hear a beautiful song. It's embarrassing, frankly, and completely involuntary. I am physically incapable of listening to Dan Fogelberg's "Leader of the Band" without crying. I openly wept once in Rogan's Shoes when "Live Like You Were Dying" came on the overhead speakers. A few years ago at a Bonnie Rait concert, my friend repeatedly patted me on the knee to comfort me as tears streamed down my face while Bonnie crooned "I Can't Make You Love Me."

On the flip side, as a performer, I've watched audience members wipe their eyes when I sang my deepest truths. I've had people approach me after a show to tell me how much they connected with a particular song. (And sometimes they even buy the CD that contains that tune. Bonus!) I don't believe these tears deepen anyone's despair. It's therapeutic to get that out, isn't it? Whether it's the melody, the words, or the beauty of the human voice, music has the power to shamelessly tug on our heartstrings. But within that process of listening, there is a release that somehow cleanses us.

What about when you need to get pumped? Think about an athlete pacing the locker room with her earbuds in, preparing for competition. Or picture every Nike commercial ever made. (Watching commercials during the Olympics also brings me to tears. Yes, I have problems.) Listening to hard-driving music can unleash your inner animal. *And* make you want to buy running shoes, possibly even while crying in Rogan's.

Visualize a mosh pit at a death-metal concert. All that teenage angst has to be expressed somehow, right? Or an eight-month-old baby in a car seat clapping her pudgy hands to a Sesame Street sing-along during a long car ride. Or an elderly couple dancing cheek-to-cheek at their 50th wedding anniversary party to a song they loved when they first met—their children, grandchildren, and great-grandchildren looking on in amazement at all the life that sprang from that enduring love. There are countless examples of the ways listening to music helps us regulate or enhance our emotional states. We literally all have a soundtrack to our life.

Lyrics Help You "Put a Name on It"

Have you ever felt a mysterious pain in your body and wondered, "What is happening?" Suddenly your brain starts catastrophizing, "Oh, good gracious! I must have a rare and deadly flesh-eating virus of the ankle! They're going to have to amputate!" So you go to the doctor, she runs some tests and tells you that you've developed a stress fracture. Oh, phew! The pain is still there, but don't you have a sense of relief in knowing what's wrong? Putting a diagnosis on a particular physical concern gives you a prognosis, and that prognosis can give you a sense of control.

Song lyrics can have a similar effect. When a listener hears a songwriter spell out the details of their condition, it can be quite a relief. I was playing in a writers' round with two other songwriters years ago, and after a particularly heart-wrenching song, I jokingly commented to one of my stage-mates, "Man,

I think you need therapy!" After the chuckles subsided, he wisely replied, "Actually, I don't need therapy because I write songs!" My musical friend inherently knew what psychologists often teach their clients: naming your thoughts can decrease the negative emotional toll.

Think about how this can play out for a listener. Let's say you have this strange pain in your chest every time you think about your ex. You wonder if it will ever go away. One day you find yourself driving down the highway with the radio blaring and a heart full of angst. The DJ spins one of the approximately ten million songs written titled something like, "I'm Getting Over You." Suddenly, your windows are down and you're singing along at the top of your lungs. You don't freaking care that the other commuters are looking at you strangely! No! Because you realize: "Ha ha! Yes, I'm going to get over this schmuck! Just like the singer of this song did!" Chest pain? Diagnosed as a broken heart. Prognosis? Full recovery looks promising. Listening to that song helped you put a name on your issue and gave you a deeper understanding of your condition.

This is part of the reason why you hear pro songwriters say, "Write what you know." The more real you are in your songwriting, the more it will resonate with your listener. So don't just say what you *think* people want to hear. And, for heaven's sake, don't just use a lyric because it fits your rhyme scheme, if it's not what you mean to say. Work hard. Dig deep. Tell me your truth in your song. Not ironically, the most deeply personal songs I've written are often the ones that get the best feedback. The fact is, a listener doesn't need to have experienced the exact same story that the singer shares. The details can differ, but if the emotional truth is the same, *that* is when you and your listener start to vibrate at the same frequency.

Researcher Brene Brown's book, *Daring Greatly: How the Courage to Be Vulnerable Transforms the Way We Live, Love, Parent, and Lead,* extensively explores the concept of vulnerability. In her June 2010 TEDxHouston talk, she stated, "In order for connection to happen, we have to allow ourselves to be seen. *Really* seen." She goes on to state that true connection requires authenticity.[3] When Alanis Morisette released her debut album *Jagged Little Pill*, her in-your-face, confessional style of writing took the world by storm. Listening to her words felt like reading her diary. Morissette let us *really see* her and it resonated to the tune of thirty-three million copies sold.

Brown's research also wisely demonstrates that you cannot selectively numb your emotions. If you want joy, gratitude, and love, you have to experience fear, guilt, shame, and all the other icky things we'd prefer to box up and ship off. This is why people want to listen to sad or angsty songs. We have to feel *all* this stuff, my friends. We can't have the highs without the lows. Vulnerability in your songwriting can help you and your listener process all these feelings. Shoving down the tough stuff doesn't do us any favors. We have to face it. Feel it. Name it. And *then* we can move on.

When I give songwriting workshops, I often joke, "Pour your entire truth into what you write. And then if someone you wrote an unflattering song about asks you, 'Is this song about me?' *that* is when you lie." Of course, honesty is the best policy in life, folks, but, I'm just sayin', safety first.

Now, on the flip side, not all listeners care about the lyrics.

Gasp! I know, if you're a word-nerd like me, this is a hard pill to swallow. But the truth is, some people love the music they love based strictly on a *feel*.

My husband, Tony, has been my drummer since 2002. We put out our first album back in 2004 with our band, Clear Blue Betty. One of the songs on the album tells the story of how we fell in love, how he fills my heart, and is still the man of my dreams. Two years after we released that record, we happened to be listening to that song. He tilted his head to the side and sincerely inquired, "Is this song about me?"

"Whaaaaaaatttttt??????!!!!!!!"

In his defense, poetry can be confusing. And drums are really loud. But, I mean, c'mon!!! How could he not know? Well, frankly, because he's not into the lyrics like his literary-snob wife. So, if you're the kind of person who doesn't think that hard about what you have to say when you write, but you totally get into the groove, you may be Tony's next favorite artist. (All kidding aside, Tony does actually listen to lyrics. . . sometimes.)

We all have our reasons for listening. These reasons can vary for each person from day to day and setting to setting. Some people just enjoy listening to gifted, passionate performers. Adele could sing the phone book and some of her fans would eat it up because of her incredible voice. Robert Plant of Led Zeppelin could have sung the recipe for beef stroganoff and I'm confident some fans would still bang their heads. So understanding that people listen for completely different reasons can be quite liberating. I'm not suggesting that you deliberately compromise your lyric writing or purposely sing lyrics you don't believe. I'm just saying that it's helpful to understand that lyrics aren't the be-all-and-end-all for every listener.

Live vs. Recorded Listening

Speaking of performers, live music is a different animal than recorded music. What's the difference for our audience when it comes to listening to a recording versus a live performance? This is certainly something to consider if you're a performer who also wants to sell records.

I've heard songs on the radio that have inspired me to go out and buy the singer's album. Then I bought a concert ticket and fell out of love with the music because the performer did something that turned me off. In 2008 I went to a concert (of a band-who-will-remain-unnamed) and the lead singer literally brought a small tree onto the stage, stopped the whole concert and refused to start singing again until someone in the crowd could correctly identify the tree. Seriously? I still can't listen to their music without thinking of the twenty-four minutes of my life that the singer wasted because of a pomegranate sapling. I've also had performers make me fall even deeper in love with them and their music when I saw their live performance. When a performer has charisma and authenticity, it can be absolutely intoxicating. KT Tunstall kills me every time! She's hysterical, uber gracious, and so freaking talented. I love her. The moral of the story is you have a unique advantage during a live performance to draw your listener in on a completely different and deeper level.

I often feel my entire musical career is built on this. I'm not a highly trained, flawless guitarist or singer, but when I am on stage, that is my happy place. I am usually able to make up for my lack of skill as a vocalist or instrumentalist by being a dynamic performer and a good storyteller. I am also genuinely grateful that people come to my shows and I try to let them know that. There's still an occasionally insecure artist living inside of me that is amazed anyone would want to hear me, so when I see someone getting into something I've created, I am honestly touched that they want to listen. That gratitude becomes a positive energetic loop between me and the audience.

Part of the reason that the stage is my happy place is that I love to move with the music. And it's not just for show. If I have the space, I bang my head at rehearsals. It is authentically me to kick my leg at the cut off and drop to my knees when my guitarist plays a blistering solo. I love the feeling of "having left it all on the stage" at the end of a show. From the crowd's perspective, I think it's gratifying to see someone "in the zone." It's why there's a multimillion dollar sports industry and we idolize elite athletes. It's thrilling to live vicariously through watching another human pull off an inspired performance.

From the listener's perspective, part of the beauty of a live musical performance, in comparison to witnessing something like a theatrical production, is that musical performers can break down that proverbial "fourth wall." As a songwriter, I love being able to interact with the audience and share a brief glimpse into the inspiration behind a piece. It can be as simple as saying, "This is a song about forgiveness," before launching into a tune. Your listener's interest might be piqued by this brief statement. I can't tell you the number of times people have come up to me after a performance and said something along the lines of, "I can't remember the name of the song, but that one that you said was about your husband. . .I love that one!" You've probably heard the expression, "People won't remember what you said, but they will remember how you made them feel." Well, it's partly true. People will remember a bit of what you said, if your words connect with them on an emotional level. Again, our listeners want to feel connected to something, and your live performance can provide that connection.

In contrast, let's talk about the experience of listening without the benefit of the performer standing in front of you. An artist in a recording studio typically doesn't have the advantage of a live audience to give them a boost. Heck, many times the artist doesn't even have the advantage of having her bandmates nearby to pull from energetically, as today's recordings are often pieced together based on who in the band can make it to the studio on what day to record their part. Learning to channel your emotions in a studio performance setting is a precious skill. And that skill can have a profound impact on the way a listener perceives your recorded music. Obviously, a good engineer who captures the right sound and mixes the music well will impact this too. But if you're singing or playing into a microphone in an isolation booth with the audio engineer as your sole audience member, you have to learn to tap into something deeper inside you and sing with emotion so that your listener feels you.

From the listener's perspective, hearing a song on headphones allows a different kind of analysis of the music. Growing up, I remember a little white boombox I had with a radio and cassette tape player. I'd wait for the DJ to spin a favorite tune and I'd record them from the radio to a blank cassette (yes, the classic mixtape). I'd listen over and over to certain tunes, memorizing the lyrics and singing along. The beauty of having a recording and being able to listen in the privacy of your own home is that no one looks at you like you're a freak for singing into your hairbrush. Many listeners want to interact with the music in a more private setting. They want to dance, play air guitar, or pretend that they are on stage singing their hearts out to hundreds of adoring fans. For some listeners music isn't just a spectator sport, which brings me to my next point about why people listen.

Expanding and Stimulating Our Brains

As a species, human beings have continuously found ways to activate and expand the capacity of our brains. The rise of civilization and technology depends on this. Art is just one method in which we engage our inherent need for cognitive expansion. Taking in art stimulates our senses. Walking through an art gallery challenges our brains with new visual stimuli. Studying the colors, shapes, and textures tickles our nerve endings and captures our imaginations. Taking in music certainly stimulates the senses. The sounds, lights, and vibration through our bodies sends electrical signals through billions of neurons protected beneath our cranium. These impulses literally reshape a listener's brain.

The need for mental stimulation is very different for different listeners. Some people geek out on songs that change tempos and time and key signatures eighteen times over the course of five minutes. Other people just want to tap their foot to an easy country waltz. There is no right or wrong way to listen.

Distraction vs. Living in the Moment

I've taken some informal polls amongst my five thousand FaceBook friends about why they listen to music. Many replied that it provides a distraction. I have a philosophy on that, though. I think it's less about distraction and actually more about being *in the moment.* Being in the moment has its benefits. That is why it's so intoxicating to be in love. When you're in the company of someone with whom you're totally smitten, time seems to stand still. You are just so *with* that person that the rest of the world ceases to exist. Floating in all that nowness is a lovely experience.

We humans have a propensity to spend a lot of time ruminating on the past or fantasizing about the future. Music brings listeners into the present. So, sure, it *is* a distraction from your ruminations, but I believe it's really more about being in the moment with the music. When your mind is focused on the tune that's playing, it can snap you out of the often uncomfortable mental toggle between our occasionally regrettable past and our uncertain future.

You can use this to your advantage as a performer. Inviting your audience to put away their cell phones and simply soak in the moment with you is quite a lovely invitation. And it's much more heartening to see a crowd with its eyes glued to you, than it is to see everyone looking down at their phones.

So there are all sorts of reasons people listen to music. Probably plenty that I've failed to list here, but following are some take-home points for you, my dear songwriter:

- With so many different reasons to listen to music,

there's no need to ever say, "If only I sounded like *that*, then everyone would love me." It's not possible for one song or one artist to be universally loved. Take the pressure off yourself. Find your voice and then find the people who like it.

- Recognize that the music you create is a gift. Recognize that the music *anyone* creates is a gift. Stop judging yourself. Stop judging others. You do you. If someone creates music and it doesn't resonate with you, it doesn't make it crap. It just means that what you are looking for as a listener is not what they happen to be delivering. And if you create music that doesn't resonate with certain listeners, it's not that you suck. It's just that you haven't found the right listeners yet. Keep searching. Keep creating. Keep putting yourself out there and sharing your gifts.

- While we probably could survive as a species without music, we have evolved as creative beings who seek out opportunities for connection and growth. Listening to music provides us with emotional and mental stimulation and opportunities to deepen awareness of our human interconnectedness.

Makes you want to turn on the radio, doesn't it?

Chapter 1: Why People Listen to Music
Too Long, Didn't Read (TLDR) Summary

Deepening your understanding of why people listen to both recorded and live music will help broaden your perspective as a musician. People take in music for a variety of reasons:

- It provides human connection.
- It helps with emotional expression and regulation.
- It puts a name on the emotions or thoughts we hold and deepens personal insight.
- It provides cognitive stimulation.
- It helps us return to the "now" and live in the moment.

With all of these reasons that people listen to music, it's foolhardy to believe you can create art that will appeal to every single person on the planet. So set judgements aside and recognize all music has its own purpose.

Chapter 1: Why People Listen to Music
Assignments

1. Poll 5-10 friends, family, coworkers, classmates, or acquaintances on why they listen to music.
2. Explain how music connects you to three different people in your inner circle. How have your mutual musical experiences created a bond (e.g., attending concerts, playing, singing, dancing, etc.)?
3. Name 3-5 songs that you love and that are connected

to a specific memory/time in your life. Outline your emotional connection to those songs by describing how you feel when you hear them. Outline specifically how your body is reacting (e.g., my eyes water, a smile creeps across my face, I feel an ache in my chest etc.).

4. If you listen to music for therapeutic reasons, explore specific physical changes in your body the next time you listen. Some questions to consider: Do you feel a shift in your breathing? Does the tension in your body or your posture change? Does your pain level fluctuate? Is there anything else that you notice happening?

5. If you are a performer with an upcoming show, write and rehearse a brief (1-5 sentence) "script" to explain the inspiration behind your original tune(s) and use this script before you begin your song(s). You don't need to recite your script verbatim when you perform, but having a plan will help you succinctly capture your song introductions.

CHAPTER 2

WHY YOUR BODY, MIND, AND SPIRIT MATTER

You take your problems to
a god, but what you really
need is for the god to take
you to the inside of you.
—Tina Turner

In chapter one, we explored why people listen to music. In the forthcoming chapters, we're going to explore your personal musical journey and purpose for creating. But in between the input of listening and the output of creating, there is an important intermediary: your body, mind, and spirit.

Let's face it. The entertainment industry can be a brutal space. Sadly, there is no dearth of naysayers and haters. And sometimes even the well-intentioned can do or say things that crush our spirits. Getting your body, your head, and your heart in an as-stable-as-possible place can help you walk through the world with resilience. We all fall at some point, but it's much easier to get back up if you're standing on sturdy ground.

Yes, I can hear your thoughts: "Hold on, Beth. This is a book on songwriting. Please don't preach to me about eating broccoli and doing pilates." But here's the thing: How can you expect your muse to thrive when you've planted her in lousy soil? When you routinely neglect adequate sleep, proper nutrition, exercise, self-care, and mental health, you are out of balance. And, sure, you can point to examples of successful creative-types who gravely violated their personal well-being, but my question is: What might have they created had they taken better care? Sure, a lot of music has been inspired by self-abusive behaviors, but does it have to be? Imagine inhabiting a well-rested, well-fed, strong, and comfortable body. How much creative energy might a songwriter like that have?

Think of what Janis Joplin and Amy Winehouse might have created if their lives had not been cut short by drug addiction. I don't say this flippantly; I say this with a true sense of tragedy. Their muses died with them. Their creative force was lost. In a society obsessed with drama, these are the stories that get the most attention: brilliant young souls lost to hard living. Why do we find poetry in this? Why can't we make documentaries on megastars who lead healthy lives? Why aren't there headlines about balanced and happy pop idols? Think about it. It skews our perception on what it takes to be an artist and what it means to be a star. We need to acknowledge this bias. We need to learn to celebrate wellness and make the best choices for our body, mind, and spirit.

Being a performing musician is a quirky job compared to other professions. Can you picture this: You walk into the office at 8:00 a.m., set your briefcase down at your desk, and the CEO saunters up and she hands you a gin and tonic? Or you head to the cafeteria on your lunch break at the hospital and one of your coworkers asks if you want to roll one in their van before you head back to the clinic?

Sounds ridiculous, right? These are literally things that

happen all the time to performing musicians. And while you may get fired for doing drugs and alcohol on the premises of your day job, you're hailed as "one of the cool kids" for doing this as a musician. I'm not saying that you can never relax with an adult beverage at your gigs (if you're of age, of course!). It's obviously a different setting than corporate headquarters, but this lifestyle can easily lead to excess and abuse. So define your boundaries, know your body, and do what you need to do to stay at the helm.

I'm not going to go into detail on how much kale you should eat or how many steps you should log on your pedometer. There are tons of great resources available to guide you to a healthy lifestyle. I'm just asking you to consider this as part of your creative well-being and to realize that a jalopy won't be as easy to drive as a Ferrari. Each day you wake up and make choices. If you make time to get a little exercise, eat healthy food, spend a few moments on meditation, express gratitude, and surround yourself with healthy and positive people, you're going to get through your days in much better fashion.

Get in Tune with Your Body

As a performer, having a healthy body can save you a lot of angst. I consider my job a physically demanding one. I haul a lot of gear (if only I had roadies!) so I need to be able to bend, stretch, pull, lift, and carry—and that's just me trying to get my Takamine out of the back of my vehicle! Singing requires a healthy lung capacity, flexible rib cage, and robust vocal chords. Playing guitar taxes my neck, shoulders, wrists, and fingers. And if you happen to be a more athletic performer, you'll have to stay flexible for your high kicks and backbends. Staying physically fit makes all these things easier. For me, it's a combination of working out to stay strong and flexible, eating well to fuel my body with replenishing nutrients, and sleeping to allow for rest and repair that keeps me thriving on the stage.

Because I'm in tune with my body, I can quickly tell when things get out of whack. Maybe I ate too much greasy food or had too much alcohol and then I feel my vocal chords suffer. Or I slack off on my workouts and I can tell it's harder to haul my gear and my back and shoulders start to ache. Or I've had one too many nights of sleep deprivation and suddenly I can't remember how to play my songs. Learn to read your body's cues and remedy the situation with self-care and better choices.

Now, I am a realist. I am well aware that there are times where life will be out of balance. Illness, death of a loved one, family crises, or big life changes like a move, a divorce, a new marriage/relationship/baby, or perhaps a global pandemic will make balancing your life a more difficult task. I also admit I'm far from perfect. So far from perfect. There have been times I've made poor decisions and lost balance, but I strive to make these less-than-stellar choices the exception and not the rule. You can do the same. It requires surrounding yourself with people who can support you and seeking out a mental health professional when necessary.

Community Matters

Let's explore the concept of surrounding yourself with the

right people a bit further. In your creative journey—and heck, in your life—if you are flanked by people who inspire you, support you, lift you up, express gratitude, and challenge you to be your best self, it's much easier than being stuck in the midst of a bunch of soul-leeching jerkfaces. Seeking out like-minded and healthy creative partners is crucial. Sometimes a bit of pruning and replanting is necessary. Extracting yourself from toxic relationships isn't easy, but it can have a wondrous effect on your music and many other areas of your life.

One thing I've learned though, is that it helps to *be* the kind of person you want to attract. My son, Gus, reminded me of this when he was just eight years old. He had a classmate whom he frequently complained about as being "annoying." He'd often hop in the minivan (yes, I drive a minivan, a *rockstar minivan*, thank you very much) after the school day and give me a report on what "Greg" did to get on his nerves. I would patiently listen and tell him he should just try to avoid the kid. But one day I picked him up from school and he reported, "I've been being nice to Greg and we're getting along a lot better." Whoa. Leave it to a third grader to be smarter than his mother.

As the Music Director of Girls Rock Camp Madison (GRCM), one of my jobs is to hire all the summer staff. I fully embrace the concept "Get the right people on the bus" taught by *Good to Great* author James Collins.[1] GRCM is a camp where kids learn about music and songwriting, but it's really more about empowerment and collaboration. So, in my hiring practice, I'm much more concerned about whether a candidate demonstrates understanding of the mission than if they're the world's biggest rockstar. I need to get the right people "on my bus" who uphold the ideals of the camp.

In my songwriting and performing career, I have worked to surround myself with people who nurture and challenge me. I have also tried to be that kind of person to my colleagues. Again, I'm human and so are my friends. It doesn't mean I'm not going to have a prima-donna moment and that my musical collaborators are always shiny-happy people. That's just not a fair expectation of anyone. But if I'm surrounded by people who make regular deposits into my emotional bank account and I do the same for them, we're all much more likely to forgive occasional diva moments.

Questions to Ask Yourself

Here are some questions I want you to contemplate on your journey in order to get the best creative output from your body, mind, and spirit:

Could I be in better physical health? If yes, what is one step I can take to feel better in my one precious gift of a body?

Suggestions:
- Reduce/quit drugs and alcohol.
- Explore healthier eating habits with a trusted medical professional.
- Work on a physical fitness plan in consultation with your doctor.

Could I be in better mental health? If yes, what is one step I can take to get my head in a better place?

Suggestions:

- Meditate.
- Seek out a counselor.
- Contemplate/construct a personal mission statement to determine if you're making choices in accordance with your values (more on this in chapter four.)

Could I be in a better place spiritually? Am I surrounding myself with people who love, support, nurture, and inspire me? If not, what is one step I can take to make this happen?

Suggestions:

- Find "your people" by joining a songwriting group or starting one yourself!
- Seek a spiritual advisor through a church, synagogue, etc.
- Find books, podcasts, speakers, etc. that inspire you to be your best self.

One last thought on this topic of body, mind, and spirit health: it's a journey, not a destination. You can't just do this for a week and be done for life. There are days when I suck at balance and days when I rock it. There are times where I'm pumping my fist in the air and celebrating how much I have my life figured out, and then the next morning something happens and I begin to question the meaning of life. You can't have the light without the dark. Be willing to sit through the hard stuff, name it, allow it, explore it, and grow. This is all part of the glorious human experiment. It's great stuff to write songs about as well.

Chapter 2: Why Your Body, Mind, and Spirit Matter
Too Long, Didn't Read (TLDR) Summary

Creativity thrives in fertile soil, so tend your personal garden for a healthy body, mind, and spirit. Life will have its ups and downs, but surrounding yourself with people and resources to get you back on your feet when you fall off balance can enhance and prolong your songwriting journey.

Chapter 2: Why Your Body, Mind, and Spirit Matter
Assignments

1. Answer the italicized questions in the "Questions to Ask Yourself" section of this chapter. Write down one step you can take toward improving your body, mind, and spirit and place it somewhere you will see everyday.
2. Make a list of people in your community who might be willing and able to help you on your songwriting journey. Also list specific ways they might support you and a concrete plan to connect with one of them in the next week to express your desire for their support. If the first person you ask isn't able to offer support, move on to the next one.
3. Journal about your perspective on mental health and creativity. Do you fear you will lose your creative "edge" if you increase your contentment? If so, write about how improving your mental health might make creativity easier.

CHAPTER 3

GET TO KNOW YOUR SONGWRITER ORIGIN STORY

Now that we've explored why people listen to music and the importance of body, mind, and spirit balance, I want to give you some tools to help you understand what motivated *you* to embark upon a songwriting journey. It doesn't matter if you haven't written a song yet, or if you have been writing for years; getting a grasp on your songwriter origin story can help you uncover your true self. We will explore your personal "whys" for creating music in the next chapter, but right now let's look at how you got into music, or maybe more correctly, how music got into you.

With the hope that it provides some insight into your own history, I want to share a bit on who I am and how I got to where I am in my musical life today. If your brain works anything like mine, you might want to know more about "the woman behind the mirror." For whatever reason, when I pick up a book or hear an intriguing new artist on the radio, I want to know more about the originator of the work. What do they look like? Where do they come from? What's their story? Getting to know people is kinda my thing. I don't want us to be strangers.

So, if you're willing, take some time to read my story. At the end of this chapter, I will give you some prompts to write your own.

My Songwriter Origin Story

I am the offspring of a poet-actress-singer supermom and a multi-instrumentalist, tire salesman, entrepreneurial master gardener dad. Music was ever-present in the modest house where I was raised in northern Wisconsin. I remember my mom, Sue, rehearsing songs for community plays, where she starred in roles like Marion the Librarian in *The Music Man* or Anna in the *King and I*.

In addition to seeing my mom sing and act on stage when I was a kid, she would also share her poems, many of which were published in magazines. My little brain found it downright nifty that you could get your words and name in print like that. Mom held poetry meetings at our house from time to time with some of her creative counterparts. I never sat in on the meetings, but I learned that artist types like to congregate and share their works.

Inspired by my mom, I wrote a lot of poetry as a kid. Not too long ago, my mom handed me a folder of my grade school musings. (Thanks, Mom, for keeping that!) I was no Maya Angelou, but it wasn't bad for a first-grader. It was fun to read seven-year-old Beth's musings about the world. So my love of word-play began quite young.

I also was lucky enough to have a piano in my house growing up. My formal music instruction began when I started piano lessons at four or five years old. Before you get too impressed, the lessons only lasted a few months. My most vivid memories of those lessons are of my instructor's poorly groomed sheepdogs, who would come and breathe their stinky biscuit breath on my little body while I played. I didn't quit because of the canines, though (and I have evolved into a dog lover). My teacher passed away and that was the end of my piano lessons. I still had the piano at my house, fortunately, and continued to plunk around on it because I simply enjoyed it.

Mom may have provided my love of words and penchant for the stage, but it was my papa who brought me the rhythm. My dad, Bob, always has a tune playing in his head. Mom jokingly refers to this internal radio station as "WBOB." I can still hear his fingers tapping "Wipe Out" on the dining room table and see him from my perch in the backseat, mentally playing his long-lost high school drum kit on the steering wheel to whatever tune was on the car stereo. He also had a rusty, old trombone in his closet that he tried to play for us once or twice (man, that was *loud*!), and when we'd visit my grandparents, he and grandpa would bust out the old accordion and play waltzes by ear. I can still picture my dad and me sitting at our piano. He'd show me where to put my fingers and we'd play boogie-woogie tunes. There was never any sheet music involved. It was all just based on listening and feeling the groove.

My parents definitely were my earliest and most influential musical and creative role models. I was never discouraged from expressing myself and for this I am forever grateful. Speaking of expressing myself, I spent a fair amount of time in my youth singing into my hairbrush (or a red plastic maraca, as I vaguely recall). I can still vividly see the turntable and album covers for Dan Fogelberg, Michael Jackson, Cyndi Lauper, Air Supply, Barbra Streisand, the BeeGees, Donna Summer, and the Pointer Sisters. I loved to dance and sing along. I geeked out on being able to sing all the words printed on the album sleeves.

Fast forward to sixth grade, where I picked up the clarinet. Having had some musical background, I took to the instrument pretty quickly, which was highly rewarding. It made me feel special, like I had some skills. I truly loved making music, so I never had to be browbeaten by my folks to practice.

During our summer lessons, we were given the assignment to write a little tune. I still remember writing those notes on the page. I remember some of my classmates having a really hard time with it, despite being capable players. I didn't think much of it at the time, but that was likely the first time that I realized that not everyone hears melodies in their heads. I was kind of a weirdo.

I started going to summer band camps. (Yes, please feel free to insert *American Pie* quotes here.) My first summer at the senior session of band camp, I was one of the youngest kids placed in the most advanced level band. I sat in the second to last "chair" in that clarinet section, but I was still pretty amazed to have made it. It was hard, though. The kid who sat first chair in the clarinet section happened to be from my hometown. He seemed like a musical demigod to me. I still remember telling him that I didn't think I'd ever be able to play the hard passages, but he told me I'd get there. He was right.

Fast-forward to my senior year of high school; I was a complete and utter band nerd by that time. I practiced my clarinet and saxophone *a lot*. I mean, like, queen of the band geeks. But I loved music. It was work, but at the same time, it wasn't work, y'know? Despite a passion for music, somewhere along the line, I convinced myself that I could never make a living making music and I truly was interested in psychology. So I went to the

University of Wisconsin–Madison to get my psychology degree, thinking that I could solve all the world's problems, one client at a time.

Despite abandoning the idea of being a music major, I still wanted to be involved with music, so I auditioned for, and thankfully got into, the UW Marching Band. Holy buckets! Talk about being "with your people." I felt more at home with this group of people than I'd ever felt anywhere else. It was physically and mentally demanding and took up a ton of time, but when I was on the field with those musicians I was in the zone.

My senior year of college, I was all set to start applying to grad school in psychology but I just . . . could . . . not . . . do . . . it. Feeling a little panicked, I started to explore other options. One of my college roommates was working toward a degree in occupational therapy and suggested that I check out physical therapy. I did some volunteer work with some awesome PTs and really dug it. So I spent another year as an undergrad completing prerequisites for the graduate program and was lucky enough to get in the next year.

Grad school was pretty time consuming and it was the first time in my life that I wasn't involved in musical performance. From June until December of 1997, I was basically either in class or studying at the library. At the end of my first fall semester, I was invited to go to a Christmas concert at my friend's church during final exams week. I desperately needed a break, so I agreed. I was expecting a bunch of eight-year-olds singing sappy songs about Jesus, but instead this church had some seriously amazing people making some seriously amazing music. I sat in the back of the church and cried like a freak. This concert made me realize that I might literally die without music in my life. I was fortunate enough to have been paired with a wonderful woman named Judy as my PT program advisor, who served as a professional mentor and psychotherapist to me. At one of our advisor sessions, I tearfully confessed to her that I was losing my mind without music. She suggested I take up the guitar (she played a bit herself). Little did she know that this would lead to the eventual demise of my PT career. (Sorry, Judy.)

I didn't have a ton of time to mess with the guitar until I graduated, but once I finished school, I spent more time with it. Just for fun-sies. I took a few lessons, but I was mostly self-taught. (*Guitar For Dummies* became my BFF.) I also knew that I wanted to put words to music. I really didn't have much formal vocal training; I was in middle school choir, but nothing after that. I loved to sing but had a lot of doubts when it came to my voice, some of it justified, some of it a product of perceived put-downs from high school classmates who gave me funny looks for singing on the bus on the way to basketball games. At this point, I wasn't really that worried about it since I was only singing and playing to myself in my bedroom.

Enter Andy, a PT patient of mine (who has given me permission to write this; thank you, HIPPA) who came to me with a shoulder he injured hauling a guitar amp. During our treatment sessions, I mentioned that I was teaching myself to play and had written a couple songs. He said I should join a group of songwriters he had assembled that jammed at his house a few times per month. Not wanting to cross a professional line, and feeling reluctant to share my creations, I declined.

Fortunately, several weeks after Andy's treatment sessions ended he called me again to say, "Hey, you should join us!" I was nervous as heck, but I did it. And I am eternally grateful to that kind and supportive group who encouraged and taught me so much. We morphed into a band for a short time, which gave me the opportunity to perform with my guitar and voice for the first time. Despite being nervous, I knew I loved being on stage and wanted to keep doing it.

Another person who deserves a ton of credit in my songwriting career is my husband, Tony. He and I share a love of music. (We started dating while we were both in the UW Marching Band.) Much like my dad, Tony was constantly drumming on desktops, except he had an actual pair of drum sticks (despite the fact he never had an actual set of drums). A couple of years after I picked up the guitar, I enlisted the help of family and friends to buy him a drum kit as a graduation present. At his graduation party, I sent him on a wild scavenger hunt around the neighborhood near our first home, while my dad assembled the kit we'd all purchased. I think he was pretty shocked when he returned and found a shiny new drum kit set up in our basement. Thus began our musical collaborations. I'd play my guitar and sing and he'd rock out on the kit. We were both clueless, but we made time to practice when we weren't busy with our day jobs.

We were fortunate enough to hook up with a couple of musicians who knew more than we did: enter Rob Koth on guitar and Doug Sies on bass. Rob was married at the time to one of my former PT classmates, Christine, who helped manage the band, and Doug was the bass player in my first songwriting group with

Andy. We started writing songs and figuring out the whole "being in a band" thing. In 2002, we booked our first gig with our new band Clear Blue Betty and played to our amazingly supportive friends and family. Were we awesome? Heck no. Did we keep going, learning, and growing along the way? Absolutely.

During my time with Clear Blue Betty, I was highly motivated to improve my craft as a writer, so I joined a couple of different songwriting circles. One was the Madison Songwriters Group, led by Eric Hester. Eric organized a monthly meeting to share songs and get feedback. He also taught classes that gave me a ton of tools for writing. Looking back, I think it was the first time I realized that great songs weren't just magical creations funneled through humans by the divine. Great songwriters could be built! How exciting!

I also joined the Nashville Songwriters Association International (NSAI). This was another awesome resource to learn more about the music business and song crafting. NSAI held conferences and workshops in Nashville throughout the year. Madison seemed like a pretty musical town to me, but Nashville was a different planet. The trips I made to that town really opened my eyes to the industry, in all its glory and all its warts. This is also where I came to realize that there are famous singers who don't write their own songs. I mean, I think I knew this at some level, but I didn't realize how the business piece of it worked. The fact that a songwriter could make money by having someone famous sing their song was rather intriguing to me. I was in my thirties when I started making these Nashville trips. And somewhere along the way I convinced myself I was too old to be a young and famous artist, so this idea of letting someone younger, prettier, and more talented sing my songs seemed attractive.

After several years of working full time as a physical therapist and being in a part-time band, I decided to take a baby step and cut my day job hours in half. This allowed me more time for band business as well as creating and learning. Several months later, my husband was offered the opportunity to do a year of training in Texas. We uprooted from southern Wisconsin to Houston and I decided to quit my day job for good. Taking that leap was terrifying. There were voices in my head telling me it was selfish, ridiculous, impractical, and that everyone would think I was crazy. But there were louder voices saying, "You know you will regret it for the rest of your life if you don't at least try." Saying goodbye to work colleagues and my bandmates in Clear Blue Betty was difficult and sad, but also felt like the right move.

Now, I did have the luxury of being with a very supportive partner, both emotionally and financially on this journey, and that definitely made the transition easier, so I can't pretend that I was living in a cardboard box and eating ramen noodles during this time. Making this big leap in Texas was actually a gift, as the music scene in that state is a model for what the rest of the world should be doing. But I had to be extremely focused and disciplined since my days were now unstructured. No one handed me a schedule at the beginning of each day telling me what to do each hour of my day.

Ironically, the first month of my life without the interference of a day job was a surprisingly unproductive time for me as a songwriter. I knew it was because my brain was overwhelmed with the transition. I used to get tons of ideas for songs while driving or hiking with my dog, but with the move, my attention shifted to just trying not to get lost on the way to the grocery store. I persisted through this period. I got up early every day, took our black labrador, Buddy, out for a jog, and then got to work. I took an online publishing class through Berklee. I joined a local writers group. And once my muse returned, I wrote furiously, took voice lessons, booked gigs, found cowriters/ collaborators, and made frequent trips to Nashville. In addition to writing songs for me to sing, I was also writing songs with the intention of "pitching" them to publishers, in hopes of finding some megastar to sing one of my tunes and make me rich and famous.

While writing songs with the intention of having others perform them was an interesting exercise, I honestly could never quite get my head around it. And my heart wasn't fully in it either. Looking back on it, the allure was pretty much all wrapped around the prospect of making a lot of money. (A number one hit song can completely change a songwriter's life.) And if I could make a truckload of money with a song, then I could figuratively turn around and flip off all my demons and say, "See! Quitting my lucrative day job was totally smart!"

After my husband's training in Texas wrapped, we moved back to Madison. It was such a glorious sensation to come back home to Madison, but simultaneously disorienting to have to redefine myself as a solo artist. I had been influenced and deeply touched by a mentor I met in Texas by the name of Connie Mims. Connie was the rockin' fairy godmother of the Houston area music scene, who seemed to thrive on giving others opportunities to learn and grow in their music making. I really wanted to do what I could in Madison to create opportunities for people to be inspired through music. So, in addition to doing my own music performance, I sought out ways that I could get others on the stage too. One of those ways was Girls Rock Camp. I co-founded the Madison version of this summer camp in 2010, where we provide 8–18 year-olds with an instrument, teach them how to play it, help them write a song, and then have a showcase where they perform on a big stage for hundreds of screaming fans.

It took me a few years, but it finally dawned on me that my purpose as a creator of music was not to make a lot of money writing songs for other people. It was to inspire others through music to get in touch with their own creativity. It's funny how it took a bunch of kids banging on drums and jumping around with guitars for it all to click. They weren't making music to make money. They didn't know the "rules" of songwriting or care about publishing deals. They just wanted to rock out because it made them feel good. So I stopped making trips to Nashville and just went back to writing from the heart.

I also realized that I wanted to be as much like my Houston friend, Connie, as possible. I knew I loved to be on stage myself, but I got a huge charge out of collaborating with great people and by watching others find their zone on stage. So I just started doing things that were in alignment with these passions. There were definitely frustrations and hard lessons along the way but, man, have I ever learned a lot.

One of the first things I started when I got back to Madison was the Chick Singer Night chapter here—a quarterly showcase to give women at all stages of their careers the chance to sing with a killer backup band. (I later changed the event title to "Sing It Sister.") I created and led an after-school "Song Crafter's Club" for a couple years at a local high school. I helped to co-found (with my friend Erik Kjelland) an annual Americana music festival called Flannel Fest that features local and regional bands in two different cities. I also worked as the Executive Producer of the Madison Area Music Association (MAMA) Award show (Madison's version of the Grammys) and designed and opened my own home studio, where I specialize in recording projects for musicians who are new to the studio experience.

In addition to my own band, I also joined forces with two of my best friends (two incomparable women by the names of Shawndell Marks and Jen Farley) to create a trio called Gin, Chocolate & Bottle Rockets, which does motivational speaking in addition to performing. And I formed another band called Kerosene Kites with my Flannel Fest co-founder, Erik, who happens to be one of my favorite songwriters. In the midst of all these projects, I was trying to be a good mom to my son, Gus, who was born in February 2011.

In March 2020, when the pandemic shuttered venues and shifted our kiddos to school at home, like many people, I struggled mightily. My identity was largely tied to running around like a chicken with my head cut off. Not being able to make music with my bandmates for audiences felt like losing a soulmate. But being forced to slow down was also a bit of a wake-up call to me. There were definitely things I was doing to be the hero, and I was playing the martyr far too often. I was not a consistently levelheaded mother and I was rarely truly present with my family. That was a tough pill to swallow for someone who prided herself in having it all figured out. It took a lot of meditation, reading, yoga, conversations with friends, antianxiety meds and, yes, songwriting, for me to get to the place where I am now.

I will forever be a work in progress, but I feel like I've narrowed my life down to the things that feel most essential: Motherhood. Girls and Ladies Rock Camp. Performing. Songwriting. My studio. Still plenty of irons in my fire, but I've let several things go that were draining my time and energy for the things that fill me the most.

As for the songwriter in me, she's less concerned about proving herself and more into using music as a tool for self-discovery, healing, collaboration, and connection.

So that is a synopsis of my musical journey. Now it's your turn to get out the paper and pen or open up the laptop. You can simply start telling your life story or you can look below for prompts that may help you uncover your songwriter origin story.

Writing Your Own Songwriter Origin Story

It can just be some bullet points on paper but, seriously, write your story. Get to know who you are and you may start to understand your motivations a bit better. It's alright to feel all the emotions as you walk through this process: loss, triumph, shame, pride, embarrassment, joy. Let it all flow through you.

Questions you could answer to document your story:

- What are my earliest musical memories?
- What influence did my family have on my music?
- What formal musical training did I have?
- What informal musical training/experiences did I have?
- What are my most memorable musical experiences as a spectator and/or a performer?
- When did I first start collecting song ideas (melodies, lyrics, musical motifs , etc.)?
- When did I write my first song? (If you haven't yet written a song, ask: "Why am I drawn to songwriting?"
- What motivated me to write that first song?
- When did I perform my first song? How did that feel?
- Who has influenced me musically?
- What am I doing musically when I feel most "alive" and "in the moment/flow/zone?"
- If you stepped away from music at some point in your life and are now returning to it, ask yourself: "What makes me want to prioritize music right now?"
- What does my negative self-talk tell me I should do with my musical ideas?
- How can I gently thank that negativity for attempting to protect me and gently usher it to the back seat?
- Who in my community can I seek out to help me build up my musical/songwriting muscle?

I hope this journey of self-discovery has helped you. We'll do one more deep dive in the next chapter that will help you to craft your personal musical mission statement.

Chapter 3: Get to Know Your Songwriter Origin Story
Too Long, Didn't Read (TLDR) Summary

Knowing your songwriter origin story helps you tap into the most authentic version of your creative self. Your inner artist thrives when you let go of memories that diminish your creative expression and tap into the things you love about music.

Chapter 3: Get to Know Your Songwriter Origin Story Assignments

1. Answer the "Writing Your Own Songwriter Origin Story" questions.
2. What moments in your "Origin Story" stand out as the most authentic version of you, where you felt like you were in tune with your muse?
3. What moments in your "Origin Story" do you need to let go? Write them down on a piece of paper. Now, rip that paper up and throw it away.

CHAPTER 4

WHY DO YOU WANT
TO WRITE SONGS?

Now that you've written your musical past, let's turn our attention to the present. There is something about who you are that is compelling you to read this book on songwriting. You're clearly on a songwriter journey. But do you have a compass? This chapter will help you craft a personal mission statement that you can use as a compass to ensure the steps you take are in the right direction. Crafting a mission statement for your art is a critical step in approaching it with a clear head. It can help you with personal goals and expectations and it can help you ward off the demons when they decide to visit.

I mentioned in the preface that in my many forays into songwriting workshops, I've never seen one offered on *why* we write. Why is that? Well, in my humble opinion, it is because we humans spend a lot of time busying ourselves with the day-to-day and forget why the heck we even started doing whatever the heck it is we're doing. We learn all sorts of tips and tricks for getting whatever the job is "done" but lose sight of the importance of *why* we should even do the job in the first place. Can you see the problem with this? What if we're filling our lives up with things that don't resonate with our values? What does that do to our psyche?

The Nashville Hammer

Before I go too far down this rabbit hole with you, I want to share a story. There's a saying that goes "If all you have is a hammer, everything looks like a nail." It's a phrase that I heard first during my training as a physical therapist. It was meant as a warning to not make assumptions about a person's pain source based solely on my scope of practice.

Let me elaborate. If a patient came to me with low back pain, as a physical therapist, I was trained to treat musculoskeletal sources of pain. But what if the source of pain was a tumor? I couldn't personally diagnose or treat that problem, but I could broaden my awareness to ensure I didn't overlook that as a possible source.

How does this relate to songwriting? Well, as I personally became clear on why I was writing, I had an epiphany: there were some people that hit my songs with a hammer, but that wasn't always what the song needed. Basically, I learned that there was feedback that was helpful and there was feedback that I needed to scrutinize.

Becoming a member of NSAI early on in my songwriter journey provided a treasure trove of resources. This organization had loads of online classes as well as workshops to attend, led by some of the best and brightest in the industry. I learned about the craft and business of songwriting from the wonderful people involved. One additional service they offered was online access to "song critiquers" who would give you feedback on your tunes. I would submit songs for these critiques from time to time. We also had monthly meetings where fellow songwriters would share music and the group would offer suggestions they thought might strengthen your song.

While I frequently received helpful feedback, there were times I would take it in and think, "Huh?" There were some songs that I wrote with the intention of "pitching" to a Nashville publisher with hopes that they could get it into the hands of some up-and-coming country star. But there were also times I was simply writing for myself, something I could perform at my shows for my own fans. Frequently, when I took these songs in for critique, I would find that the feedback was very much focused on "Writing for the Row," meaning Music Row in Nashville, a stretch of publishing companies that had the potential to get your songs into the hands of country stars and make you rich and famous.

I watched many songwriters at these sessions get the same kind of "Writing for the Row" feedback. In my head, I dubbed the term "Nashville Hammer." It would always sadden me when I'd watch new writers join the group and then slink away with their tails between their legs when a critiquer would totally miss the point of the song they shared. Country music tends to be quite literal. It can be extremely clever and poignant, but it's not typically ambiguous. If you study the lyrics written in other genres and compare them to country, you'll likely observe a lot more ambiguity in noncountry genres. Have you ever listened to songs that were amazing, but the lyrics were so cryptic you had no clue what they were about? Yeah, that's not country; country doesn't usually leave you wondering like that.

I wish I could say I had this "Nashville Hammer" epiphany early on in my career, but it took many years of writing, figuring out my intention for my songs, gaining confidence, listening to fan feedback, getting politely pummeled, and then dusting myself off and getting back up to figure this out. And I want to be clear, just like I never had the intention of misdiagnosing a patient, I know with all my heart that these critiquers were offering their best to the songwriters who brought them their songs. But I do think, just like my failure to broaden my mind could cause me to miss the boat as a healthcare provider, that some of these critiques were done with a narrow focus and they failed to take the songwriter's intention into account.

Your Intention = Your Why

Clarity in purpose can give you peace. And let's not kid ourselves: this is not something you figure out one day and then—*voilà!*—you're set for life. You have to keep coming back to your "whys" and doing the gut check, asking questions like: "Does this still resonate with me? Am I being authentic?" I've been writing since 1999, and I can say that I'm a much different artist today than I was back then, and my purpose as a writer has evolved.

How do you figure out *your* "why"? It may sound flippant, but simply ask yourself: "What is my why?" As much as I'd love to do the work for you here, I can't. So get out a paper and pen and start journaling. Just keep asking: "Why do I want to write songs?" And don't worry if there isn't a singular answer. Life is complicated, baby. If you're like me, maybe you hear voices in your head, see lyrics jump off of billboards, hear melodies and rhythms in the gas pumps, and compose songs in your dreams.

And if you don't get them out, you feel like your head will implode.

As I mentioned earlier, I took piano lessons when I was four and that's where I learned the basics of reading music, but I discovered something wild many years later. My mom found a cassette tape of me playing piano as a five-year-old that I listened to over thirty years later. I played two songs on this recording. The first was me playing "Ave Maria" out of a lesson book. It sucked. Oops, I mean, alright, it was "nice." (Here's your pat on the head, little Beth). But the second song was one that I had composed myself, called "Emotion," and I have to say, old Beth was pretty impressed by little Beth. It was simple, but it was full of dynamics and emotion. It moved me. Huh. Turns out I have been a songwriter since kindergarten.

Some of us are just born with music, lyrics, and other creative particles flowing through our veins. We're special! Just like someone who is skilled in sports, or math, or animal tracking, or whatever. We're all born with predispositions that can be nurtured. Maybe *you* are just special, too, and your "why" is that you have a gift and you want to share it. Maybe your "why" is that writing music is therapeutic and it helps you sort through the world. Maybe your "why" is that you want to be rich and famous. No judgment here, but. . . .

Internal vs. Internalized Voices

These tricky questions may require a few years of therapy to sort through: Are the voices in your head really *your* voices? Or have you internalized some paternalistic/societal chatter that overshadows your authentic voice? This isn't the kind of stuff you tease out in an afternoon, folks. It's something that can take days, weeks, months, or years to investigate.

What I'm trying to say here is that your "why" shouldn't be about someone else's dreams or expectations for you. If you're doing this solely to make someone else love you, or gain their approval, you're gonna struggle. It has to be authentically you. That doesn't mean that seeking approval from your audience is bad. Heck, approval is important. Let's not kid ourselves here: approval can be another word for connection. For me, personally, it's all about that connection.

Think about that from an evolutionary standpoint. When people enjoy us, we have built a network of security around ourselves. The connection that I make with an audience goes beyond a simple need for approval and I know this. I know that there is an invisible energy that cycles through me and through audience members when we're all rapt in the moment. Those moments when we're all basking in that beautiful *now* are golden. That is a spiritual thing. And I know that it's not just good for me; it's good for the world. That is one of my "whys" for writing too. Music builds connections and community and this is the gift that I give *and* receive when I write.

Nancy Moran led an excellent music industry workshop in which she kept asking us why we wanted to be in the music business. It went something like this:

"Why do you want to be in the music business?"

"Well, because I like to perform."

"Why?"

"Uh, because performing makes me happy."

"Why?"

"Hmmm . . . . I guess when I share my truths through songwriting and people connect with that, it feels good."

"Why?"

"My brain hurts!"

While it may seem like a frustrating conversation with an overly inquisitive three year old, it actually helped me dig really deep. I realized for the first time that my lives as a wannabe psychologist, as a physical therapist, and as a performing songwriter all had something in common. For me, these are all careers that promote well-being. It's fairly obvious why a counselor or a PT could improve your health, but I realized that music does the same thing. Personally, when I am writing, I am putting a name on the things that are swirling around in my head and I feel like I'm being my healthiest, most vibrant version of me. When I put my most vibrant version of me into the world, the people around me flourish too. When I perform, it brings people together in the moment and that builds community. Omg! Boom! My mind was blown.

Another lovely resource that helped me get in touch with my purpose is *The Big Picture* by Dr. Christine B. Whelan.[1] It's a book geared toward folks who are about to graduate from college and want to figure out what to do with the rest of their lives, but I read this book in my forties and it was still impactful because it helped me get clear on, as the French like to say, my *raison d'etre*. Dr. Whelan's book asks readers to take stock in their values, their talents, and their passions to help find their calling. Reading this book helped me craft an ever-evolving personal mission statement that guides me: *I want to inspire those around me to lead healthy, creative lives, where they live in the moment, act with integrity, and share their gifts with the world.* Having clarity on this purpose has been amazingly helpful. It doesn't mean I never struggle or screw up. It just means I have a compass to guide me and get me back on track when I start to stray.

The Big Why vs. The Little Why: Song Purpose Types

These are my "big picture whys" for songwriting. But I've also come to realize that there are "whys" for individual songs as well. Some songs I write with the intention of rocking out with my band. Some I write to just sort through the noise in my head. Sometimes I just write because it challenges me mentally. There are times I sit down in my studio and just want to play around with weird sounds that I can make with Logic ProX on my MacBook Pro. Sometimes it's even a physical challenge, like when I'm learning a new guitar, piano, or vocal skill.

Here is a list of song types that provide potential big picture ideas behind the role of a song in your world. Remember, your song's "why" is the reason it exists. Having clarity on this helps you determine how to craft it and what feedback is useful.

You can think of this list as a menu of fancy mixed drinks and mocktails. This is by no means exhaustive, but in looking back over my catalog, I can see that many of my songs (as well as songs from artists I love) fall into one or more of these song purpose categories.

> ***The Pep Talk or Affirmation*** These songs are written for myself, someone I love, or the world in general, with reminders that life isn't always easy, but qualities like perseverance, love, or inner strength can get you through. James Taylor's "You've Got a Friend" is an example. So is Rachel Platten's "Fight Song." And, of course, songs like Eminem's "Lose Yourself" and Andra Day's "Rise Up" fit this category.

> ***The Rant*** Sometimes I just have to get stuff off my chest because people or situations bug me. Or perhaps I need to tell someone off but can't do it to their face. My rant songs keep me from saying things I will regret, prevent me from throwing punches, and remind me to speak up when necessary. The song "Common Sense" on the 2023 Beth Kille Band album *This Open Road* is a rant. One of my favorite rant songs is "Pardon Me" by Incubus.

> ***The Revelation*** Revelation songs divulge some universal truth I've come to deeply understand in life, such as "people are complicated" or "love is the answer." One popular example of this is Whitney Houston's "The

Greatest Love of All," where she details her discovery of the importance of self-love. Tim McGraw's "Live Like You Were Dying" is another revelation song that delivers the message: "Life is short, so don't waste it."

The Therapeutic   This can be a combination of a rant and revelation song. Oftentimes I write these to sort through tough relationship issues. Confession: a lot of these songs never see the light of day after I finish them, but I sing them in my head as needed for perspective. Putting a name on feelings can help you set them aside. I know this has been good for my mental health on many occasions. Adele and Alanis Morisette are masters of this kind of writing (e.g., "Someone Like You" by Adele and "Thank U" by Morisette).

The Anthem   This might be thought of as a rant mixed with a pep talk. Bruce Springsteen's "Born in the U.S.A." feels anthemic to me. Anthems are songs that motivate action or outrage in hopes of unity, change, awareness, or other lofty goals. These songs tend to generate a lot of overhead fist pumping.

The Story Song   Occasionally I feel like writing about a motivational, tragic, or sentimental experience or person. My hope with these songs is that I can impart a moral, or spin an interesting tale. I love the mini-movie that unfolds in Sugarlands' "Already Gone." You've got yourself a story song if it reads like a book that just happens to be sung and lasts less than four minutes.

The Tribute A song written for someone I love or admire, and all the reasons why, fall into the category of tribute songs. Sometimes, you just have to show your admiration! For example, Dan Fogelberg paid homage to his father in "Leader of the Band," while Elton John glorified Marilyn Monroe and, later, Princess Diana with "Candle in the Wind."

The Self-Loathing or The Regret I generally feel like I've got my life together, but there are days when I think, "C'mon, Beth. Why can't you get your stuff straight?!" Sorting through complicated feelings of self-judgment seems to be a frequent topic in heavy metal genres. The song "It's Been Awhile" by Staind is an example. If you're begging someone for forgiveness, you're probably writing for this purpose.

The Redemption Once I'm through confessing my sins in my "regret" songs, I might feel redeemed and want to write a ditty of redemption. These are tunes like Barry Manilow's "I Made It Through The Rain" or Gloria Gaynor's "I Will Survive." These songs serve to bring hope and celebrate personal triumph.

The Just For Fun-sies There are days I just can't take songwriting that seriously, so I will write a goofy song to get the crowd laughing, singing, or dancing. My

"Chapstick" song definitely falls into this category. So might songs like "Who Let the Dogs Out" or "Happy" by Pharell Williams.

The Love Song Of course, we can't forget the plain old love songs. These can be for your romantic partner but, I'll admit, I may have written a few of these for my dogs. There are just too many love songs to name and it's too obvious for me to make a list, but you probably heard at least one at the last wedding you attended. Writing to express your love is a beautiful reason to pen a tune.

The Longing Need I explain? Pining for something or someone you can't have hurts, and sometimes you just have to sing about it. Jealousy, unrequited love, or the ubiquitous "I'll Never Get Over You" tunes all fall into this category. I write these songs with the intention of sorting through grief.

The List This isn't so much the purpose of a song, but it's worth mentioning as a technique that can be used to declare your song's intention. For example, "I'm Gonna Be (500 Miles)" by The Proclaimers is a love song that lists all the things the singer would do for his love. "We Didn't Start the Fire" by Billy Joel is a rant that lists many of history's distant transgressions, to exonerate his generation from being the sole reason the world is messed up. "Good People" is a revelation song I wrote with Erik Kjelland. This tune lists all the places in the US that I've been and encountered people who are diverse, but still treat each other with kindness.

If you've done some songwriting already, do any categories resonate? If you feel trapped in one of these song purpose types, you might want to experiment with others. Create your own mix of the above ingredients, stir to perfection, and serve! Iced, hot, straight-up, paper cup, wine glass, coffee mug, fishbowl . . . go wild! One of the most beautiful things about art is that you might create it with a certain intention, but the observer can impart their own sense of meaning upon your creation. We're all just trying to make sense of the world. Sharing our experiences with one another can help us all learn and grow.

Knowing what you want an individual song to do can help you grow and expand as a writer and provide you with a way to filter feedback. If I want a song to rock the crowd, but when I perform it, no one gets up to dance, well, that's helpful feedback; I can use that to adjust and grow. Maybe I can study some songs that work for that purpose and emulate them. If I write a song to pitch in Nashville and a Nashville publisher tells me what they want to hear differently, I may want to take that advice and do a rewrite. But if I'm just writing a song for fun, for personal therapy, for posterity, or to sing to my dog, and someone comes along with a "Nashville Hammer," I can say, "Hey, it's all good, but this song is not a nail."

Having clarity on your personal "why" for making music is like building a fortress with a drawbridge. Arrows may fly at your castle, but they will fall helplessly to the ground because you will be solid within your own walls. If you know with all your heart that you're doing what you want to do, it doesn't matter if your art doesn't resonate with everyone. You. Do. You.

This fortress is not a place to isolate, though; you can, and should, invite in your allies. You can focus here on the things that fill you up. You can learn to be the kind of person you want to attract. Once you attract those people, you can open yourself up to the beautiful ways they can push you to grow. And lastly, know that your castle may be remodeled with time and that is perfectly okay. You may need to redecorate, refortify, and shake up the personnel.

For the nihilists out there who think that nothing really matters, I hear you. This probably *is* all in our heads. But that is the beauty of it. I get to decide what matters to me and I prefer to live with the philosophy that life is what I make it. Music matters to me, and if you're reading this, I bet it matters to you. So let's freakin' write some songs!

Chapter 4: Why Do You Want to Write Songs?
Too Long, Didn't Read (TLDR) Summary

Understanding your personal reasons for writing, both on a macro and micro level, gives your creative skin a protective layer. Take the time to discover how songwriting fits into your life's mission and let this guide your songwriter journey. Also, think about the purpose of individual songs you write and seek out feedback as desired from helpful and specific sources.

Song Purpose Types

You can gain perspective by taking the ten-thousand foot view of your songs to grasp why you wrote them. Here is a list of song purpose types that might help you uncover the point of your song or provide a list of outside-your-norm reasons to write:

- Give a pep talk/affirmation.
- Rant about something vexing you.
- Detail a revelation.
- Write for therapeutic purposes/to process emotions.
- Acknowledge an injustice and inspire change and action (an anthem).
- Weave a good story to impart a moral.
- Pay tribute to someone.
- Express self-loathing or regret.
- Celebrate redemption.
- Compose just for fun.
- Tell someone how much you love them.
- Lament an unfulfilled desire or longing.

Chapter 4: Why Do You Want to Write Songs?
Assignments

1. Create a draft of your personal songwriter mission statement. We'll revisit this at the end of the book, but start to think about what purpose your songwriting serves for you and the world at large.

2. Journal for ten minutes about the difference between internal (authentic) versus internalized (society-imposed) voices. How can you distinguish between these on your creative journey? Are your internalized voices positive, negative, both or neither? How can you get in touch with your authentic desires when it comes to songwriting?

3. If you've written songs, make a list of a few of them and write a one or two sentence explanation of the purpose of each song. Do they fall into one of the "Song Purpose Types" we discussed in this chapter? Or do they have their own unique categories?

PART TWO

Alrighty, people. Enough with the touchy-feely stuff. Part 2 explores song structure, song idea generation, lyric writing, melody writing, and music theory. Let's get geeky!

CHAPTER 5

SONG STRUCTURE

It may seem a bit backwards to address song structure before inspiration. I mean, don't you need to figure out *what* to write about before thinking about *how* to put those ideas in a song? There is definitely merit to that approach, and in reality, separating the *structure* of a song from the *content* of a song is something we only do in textbooks.

But here's the deal: when I ask aspiring songwriters to tell me what they are struggling with the most, I frequently hear this: "I start songs all the time, but I never finish them." People who gravitate toward writing tunes don't usually seem to have a problem coming up with ideas, but they often have a problem massaging those ideas into a completed product.

It can be quite liberating for new writers to understand that there is a method to the madness. Think of it as a potter's wheel upon which you can manipulate the clay of your song. Much like a skilled potter, you start with a big blob of clay-thoughts, then you toil for a bit at the wheel, and eventually, you mold it into a piece of art for your observer to behold.

Now, I still believe, as I stated earlier, that there are no rules in songwriting. But if you're writing folk, rock, pop, country, hip-hop, Americana, or some mish-mash of these genres, it's exceedingly rare to find an example of a song that doesn't fall into one of the song structures that appears in this chapter. So don't think of this information as "rules" for writing. Think of these tidbits as tools for putting your thoughts into a format that your listener can grasp, so you can effectively convey your song's message.

Psychologists have extensively studied how memory and comprehension work. Putting information into recognizable chunks helps with both recollection and comprehension. So having segments of your song with labels like "verse" and "chorus" aids both the performer and the listener. The repetitive nature of popular music makes it much easier to memorize, thus allowing listeners to grasp the message of your song. As a performer, it also allows you to more easily perform without sheet music.

Sadly, we've developed exceedingly short attention spans, so getting your point across in less than four minutes keeps your audience focused. As Shakespeare taught us: "Brevity is the soul of wit." This often applies in songwriting. Having a template to plop your ideas upon can keep you from rambling incoherently and losing your audience's attention. It's okay to have a song longer than four minutes, but this is usually the exception, not the rule.

And, like it or not, we have all been brainwashed to want to hear songs in familiar formats. This isn't to say that we can't love a song that has a unique structure. You absolutely have my permission (not that you need it) to deviate from the norm if it serves your song, but your audience may find some comfort in familiarity. There is still plenty of room for creativity within these boundaries.

Here's the bottom line: figure out the *intention* of your song and use *structure* to serve that. Meaning, if your song needs five verses, three bridges, and a dramatic intro, then go for it. But if you can get the job done with a familiar structure, it may be helpful to both your listener and to you as the writer-performer. And, as much as it makes me cringe when I hear instructors say, "You have to know the rules to break them," I do acknowledge that there is some merit to that.

So let's dive into some of the labels commonly used to describe the different sections of a song. One short disclaimer: as far as I know, there's no international governing body that dictates how these terms are used, so you may have learned alternate labels for the following song sections. This is my preferred system.

Verse-Chorus Variations

The most common song structure you'll hear on the radio these days is the basic verse-chorus format. We'll discuss the many variations of this format below. I'm presenting the labels of these song parts in the order they often appear, but you can think outside the box and use these different song sections in whatever order you please. We'll go through each and then look at examples to help solidify the concepts.

The Intro

Short for "introduction," the *intro* of your song is kind of like a handshake. It's your listener's first impression of the song's personality since it falls at the very beginning of the song. An intro is usually pretty short and sweet, and you've got a variety of options for how to approach it.

Instrumental Intro Maybe you greet your listener with a few chords strummed on your guitar, or with a driving drum beat that helps establish a certain expectation for how your song may behave. If the song gives you a bone crushing handshake, you can be fairly certain the band is about to melt your face. If the song takes your hand, holds onto it a bit longer than necessary, all while gazing deeply into your eyes, then you better brace yourself for seduction.

If you're playing an instrument like guitar or keyboard, the chords you choose to play in your intro often are simply the chords of the verse (see below), but sometimes songwriters mix it up and use the chords of the chorus, or some other nifty riff from the song. If you're playing with a full band or other musicians, intros can build by layering instruments gradually. Or everyone can come in all together. It's all dependent on the intention and how you want to greet your listener.

No Intro You certainly can skip the intro if it doesn't suit your song. Go ahead! Just launch straight into the singing. I will say this though: I find intros to be quite functional when it comes to live performance. If you need a moment to collect yourself and get in the groove with your bandmates, the intro can also give you a bit of breathing room to allow for all passengers to secure their seatbelts and settle in for a smooth flight. I frequently use the intro as an opportunity to saunter over to one of my bandmates and ask, "What's the first line of this song again?" Performers often strum the chords of the intro while chatting with the audience about the inspiration behind the song or sharing some other fun anecdote. This is a nice way to keep the performance moving and create a little drama.

Stand-alone Intro Sometimes the intro can have its own lyrics and chords that aren't repeated again anywhere else in the chorus. Think of "Do You Love Me" by The Contours. It starts with the words "You broke my heart 'cause I couldn't dance" and it's such a cool intro that sets the song up perfectly. It doesn't need to be repeated (it wouldn't make sense, really) and it lets the listener know exactly why the singer asks, "Do you love me now that I can dance?," in the chorus. Or think of Nancy Wilson's incredible guitar intro in the song "Crazy on You." Sister, if you've got guitar chops like that, why not show them off? This is a variation on the instrumental intro; it's not a segment of the song that is used elsewhere (meaning, it's not the verse chords or the chorus chords, etc.). It's almost like a mini-song that gets played before the rest of the song kicks in.

The Verse

Typically, the verse immediately follows the intro. Verses tend to give the details of the story within the song. Think of it as the "who, what, where, when." It's the background information that will allow the listener to grasp the main point of the song that you will get around to when you sing the chorus. My seventh grade English teacher, Mrs. Adams, told us we needed a "topic sentence" or a "thesis statement" at the beginning of our paragraphs, and that the rest of the paragraph should provide information to support that topic sentence. Think of your verses as the supportive sentences in your paragraph. The topic sentence is the chorus, which will be explained in more detail below.

Structurally, songs typically have two or three verses. You can certainly write more than three if you're super ambitious and you have enough fresh information to push the story/message forward in your song, but keep in mind that you've got to be captivating (either lyrically, melodically, vocally, instrumentally, or all of the these), so you don't lose your listener's attention. Leonard Cohen's "Hallelujah" got away with six verses, but the chorus is super simple and the lyric and delivery is stunning, so it works for that song.

Occasionally, the first verse of the song is twice the length of the second verse. If you want to think of this as verses one and two before the first chorus, and then verse three before the second chorus, that's cool with me. Having two verses before your first chorus can help you set up a little bit more of the background story before you hit your listener with the chorus. This certainly isn't always necessary. There's an adage amongst songwriters that goes: "Don't bore us, get to the chorus." So there's no harm in getting straight to the point, if that works for your tune.

The melody and chords usually stay the same from one verse to the next, but the lyrics you lay over the top of them typically change. Sometimes you'll hear singers take slight deviations from an exact melody from one verse to the next, just to show off their vocal chops or to mix it up a bit. Usually though, the basic motif of the melody is consistent from one verse to the next.

> **Second Verse Hell** I frequently encounter writers who have a verse and chorus to a song and then (dun dun duuuuun!) calamity strikes. They get stuck. This is an unfortunately pervasive phenomenon dubbed "second verse hell" that many songwriters face. If you experience this, here are some tactics that might help:
>
> 1. Move your first verse into the position of the second verse. Then write a new first verse by backing up and starting the story earlier in your imagined "timeline." For example, if you're writing a song where the first verse is about two people who are deeply, madly in love, but then you don't know what to write

about in verse two, maybe back up by telling us how these two lovers met and fell in love, and then move the deeply, madly in love part to verse two.

2. Maybe you've written a chorus with too many details and it's backing you into a corner. You may need to simplify it. Verse ideas should flow naturally into the chorus. Remember, your chorus is generally your topic sentence and your verses are the supportive ideas. If you've got too much detail in your chorus, you may need to pull some out and put them in a verse.

3. Try freewriting to get more ideas for your topic. Use all your senses to brainstorm ideas. Stop trying to write lyrics or think of rhymes and just jot down all your thoughts related to this song. Then go back and look through those thoughts for little nuggets you can turn into lyrics.

4. Find a co-writer! Two (or three) heads are better than one.

5. If your song is more groove-based and not intended to tell an epic tale, you might just keep it super simple. You could sing verse one

and a chorus and then sing verse one again! Mwahaha!

6. What if you put more space between lyrics and made them less rapid-fire? You could keep the tempo of the song the same, but stretch the melody of the words you sing, so you can split the first verse into two sections, one falling before and one falling after the chorus. Listen to Glen Hansard and Marketa Irglova sing "Falling Slowly" for a brilliant example of slowly delivered lyrics.

7. If you've tried all of the above to no avail, it's possible your idea isn't big enough for a song. So make it a haiku and get on with your life. If your heart is connected to the song you're writing, though, and you're stuck, a little time away from the writing process can give you a fresh outlook. Our brains have a wonderful way of problem-solving when we turn our attention to other tasks.

The Pre-chorus

I mentioned above that sometimes writers will have two verses before the first chorus. If you don't need an entire second verse before that first chorus hits, a pre-chorus might be your ticket. Pre-choruses certainly aren't required. Only create one if you need a section of the song to link the verse to the chorus. For example, if you want a dramatic build in the melody before the chorus hits and your verse doesn't provide that, a pre-chorus could help. Also, a pre-chorus can help if it serves as a lyrical connection between the story of the verse and the concept of the chorus. I've had drafts of songs where the message of the verse didn't quite link up logically with the chorus, so I added a bit more information in a pre-chorus, and that solved the problem.

If the pre-chorus occurs more than once in the song, the melody and chords are usually the same each time. Sometimes songwriters will even repeat the same lyrics from one pre-chorus to the next, but they certainly can change from pre-chorus one to pre-chorus two. Again, this is totally up to you. Don't choose a structure simply because you read about it in a book. Choose it because it serves the meaning of your song.

Pre-choruses can also be great if the chords of your verse and chorus are the same and you want to break those sections up to provide a break in the monotony. We'll tackle this more in depth when we get to the music theory chapter, but it's good to know about this trick so you can create some tonal variety or build some tension and release for your listener's ear. If the verse and chorus sound exactly the same, your listener may zone out and not realize you're singing a chorus, which, as we'll explore in the next section, usually contains the main point of the song. Ensuring your chorus is easily identifiable as "the chorus" can make your song more impactful.

I use this trick all the time at Girls and Ladies Rock Camps when I'm working with bands. In this setting, we've got a super short period of time to write a song, frequently working with people who are relatively new to their instruments. Writing a pre-chorus where we just break up the chord progression by holding out a chord and letting the drummer do some dramatic fill/buildup can set us up nicely for a chorus that has the same chords as the verse but ends up feeling new and different because of that pre-chorus break. We don't even necessarily add words to the pre-chorus! It could just be nonsense syllables ("la la la" or "na na na") or a sustained "ahhh." (See all these dirty little secrets you're learning?)

Sometimes, if you've just got a super-short pre-chorus, it may not *technically* be one. You might just consider this a little "lift" at the end of your verse that ramps you up into the chorus. You can call it whatever you like, just make sure it serves your song.

Check out Sarah Bareilles' "Love Song" and Adele's "Rolling in the Deep" for examples of songs with excellent pre-choruses that set the song up for killer chorus delivery.

The Chorus

The chorus is the section that usually repeats two or three times in a song with the same melody and same lyrics. Usually the lyrics in the chorus contain the "big picture" message of a song, or as I mentioned above, the "topic sentence." A chorus can be uber basic. Sometimes it's just one simple, catchy phrase repeated over and over. Think of Adele's "Rumor Has It," where she repeats the title of the song eight times! Or the Beatles' "I Wanna Hold Your Hand," where they sing the title repeatedly in the chorus.

Please place your hand on top of your nearest songbook and the other over your heart and repeat after me: "I, (insert name here), do not have to write crazy-long-winded- detailed choruses." You certainly can if you want to, but the nice thing about a simple chorus is that it makes it much easier to write multiple verses that "inform" that "topic sentence." If you write a ton of details in your chorus, you may limit your options for verse content.

Melodically, the chorus is also typically the high point of the song. Think about it: if you were speaking with someone and wanted to make sure they understood a really important point, you would speak with more emphasis. You might slow down your delivery or repeat an important sentence verbatim. The pitch and volume of your voice may raise as well. Allowing your chorus melody to preserve the natural shape of spoken language is an effective way to get the point of your song across.

The "Alternative" Chorus Occasionally, the chorus of the song changes lyrically each time you sing it. It could be as simple as a small tweak the last time you sing it, so that it takes on new meaning. One of my all-time favorite examples of a brilliant chorus tweak is the song "Stay" by

Sugarland, written by lead singer Jennifer Nettles. The song is sung from the perspective of "the other woman" in an affair. In the first two verses, she asks her lover not to leave her bed and go back to his wife, so in the chorus when she sings, "Why don't you stay?," she means, "Why don't you stay with me?" But the bridge of the song takes a twist. We hear Nettles sing that she doesn't have to live like this anymore and she sings, "So next time you find you wanna leave her bed for mine / Why don't you stay?" *Bam! Stay in your own darn bed! In your face now-ex-lover!* Mic drop. The lyrics in the final part of the song are a bit different than the first two because they now reflect her new stance.

I wrote a goofy song once called "Curves" (about how I'm flat as a pancake) where the chorus was different every time I delivered it. I did this for the sake of humor. Once you tell a joke, it loses its impact the second time, so I wanted each chorus to include new, fresh, and funny information. The melody and chords stayed the same, but the lyrics changed each time.

One of my favorite songs of all time is "Boys of Summer" by Don Henley. He subtly changes the second line of the chorus each time he sings it. The changing line is a recollection of his ex-lover's appearance. I personally think this is genius. As the listener, I feel the impact of these alternate scenes as a slow burn longing. He sees her "hair slicked back," and then sees her "walking real slow" in the next chorus, and then finally, in the last chorus, he alludes to her in her car with the "top down." Instead of giving us a single image in a stagnant chorus, it's like a minimovie unfolding. Gah! So intoxicating! High five, Don. The song came out in 1984 and I still freaking love it.

A Note about Refrain vs. Chorus If you've studied songs, you've likely come across the term "refrain." In my experience, the word is often used interchangeably with the term "chorus" and I've seen it defined as a "shorter version of a chorus that happens at the end of a verse." In my humble opinion, the distinction between a chorus and a refrain is mostly academic. Functionally, it serves a very similar purpose. It's a topic sentence of sorts. It typically comes after a verse and provides a repetitive melodic hook for your listener to bite. If you want to call it a refrain, go for it. If you want to call it a short chorus, more power to ya. I personally like to embrace the Keep It Simple, Songwriter (KISS) principle, so I'm going to stick with the term chorus. Sorry, academics. We can argue over this someday while you sip your Robert Mondavi with your pinky up and I slug down my New Glarus Brewery Spotted Cow.

The Bridge/Solo/Breakdown

I've lumped bridge, solo, and breakdown together because they all serve a similar function. These sections are all meant to be a "departure" from what you've done so far in your song. Here are brief descriptions of each:

> **Bridge** Lyrically, a bridge is a song section that often presents a new perspective. Oftentimes, it's more contemplative than the verse content. For example, if your verses outline all the troubles in your life, maybe the bridge offers a solution. Typically, it's placed before the last chorus, so that it shines a new light on the chorus, as in the Sugarland song example we explored earlier. A bridge doesn't always have to carry you over troubled waters, though. (Ha! I kill me.) It could just be a section where you chant something fun and repetitive for the crowd to sing along. At Girls Rock Camp this is frequently the section where the kids write in an opportunity to introduce each member of the band, so their parents have a chance to cheer wildly and scream, "That's my bay-bay!" I absolutely freaking love that. Melodically and chordally, the bridge should give us some fresh ear candy that breaks up the monotony of the tune. I'll share more about this in the chapters on music theory and melody, but just know for now that you may want to play new chords, play your already-used chords in a new

order, and/or introduce new melodic motifs in your bridge section.

Solo This is pretty self explanatory. If you're a skilled instrumentalist, or you've got one in your band, a solo section can be a place to showcase some chops. You can simply play the verse chords or the chorus chords and improvise over the top. Another option is to do a "bridgey" solo that has new chords as well. Go to Spotify and play Beth Kille Band's "Front Step" and you'll hear an example of a bridge that has no words, but there are new chords in the solo section that follows the second chorus. This is what I mean by a "bridgey" solo. I didn't have any other lyrical content that I wanted to deliver in a bridge, but I wanted to mix it up a bit. Plus, my guitarist Michael Tully is a fiend, so it gave him a chance to let loose. The length of this section really is up to you. You might choose to lengthen solos in live-performance settings, especially if everyone is eating it up and you want to light your guitar on fire. But just like the bridge, this section breaks up the monotony and gives your listener something new to digest.

Breakdown It's a bit of a misnomer to call this a "section" of a song, as it's more of a technique that can be applied to a section. But, again, the intention of using this technique is to add sonic freshness. Breaking a section down means stripping it back, which is typically achieved by removing some of the melodic/musical busyness and/or reducing the volume. You can apply the concept of a breakdown to a verse, chorus, pre-chorus, solo, or bridge. Frequently, it happens right before, or on top of, the final chorus.

For example, when you sing the chorus for the third time, all the instruments drop out except for the guitarist, who just does whole-note strums. Or maybe you do a third verse before the final chorus, where all the instruments drop out and you just snap your fingers in time to the beat while you sing over it. Or, if you're playing with a band, you can invite the crowd to clap overhead while you sing over the drummer laying down a simple, stripped-down beat. This technique is sooooo ever present on the radio that you probably can't go for ten minutes without hearing it. It's a lovely way to add dynamics, drama, and variety.

Verse-Chorus Variations in Action

Now that we've looked at verse-chorus variations, let's look at how you might combine them within the song structure. Once again, there are no rules in songwriting, but there is a tool songwriters use that happens to have the word rule in it. It's called "The Rule of Twos," which states that once you've done something twice in your song, you need to introduce something fresh before you repeat it again.

You've likely heard countless examples of songs that go like this:

Intro
Verse 1
Chorus
Verse 2
Repeat Chorus
Bridge
Repeat Chorus

Katie Perry's "I Kissed a Girl" fits this format. Do you hear how the bridge comes in before the chorus hits us the third time? That's an example of the Rule of Twos. I wrote a song called "End of the Line" for my 2012 solo album *Dust* that follows this format.

There are also lots of songs that go like this:

Intro
Verse 1
Pre-chorus 1
Chorus
Verse 2
Pre-chorus 2

Repeat Chorus

Guitar solo

Repeat Chorus

"Front Step" by Beth Kille Band follows this format. "Before He Cheats" performed by Carrie Underwood and "Perfect" by Pink are other examples.

And then there is this version of verse-chorus formats:

Intro

Verse 1

Chorus

Verse 2

Repeat Chorus

Guitar solo

Repeat Chorus with "breakdown" technique applied

Repeat Chorus with all instruments

I could keep going here, but hopefully you get the point. Go to your favorite streaming app, listen to songs, and see if you can hear the structure. If you do an internet search for song lyrics to your favorite songs, these sections may already be conveniently labeled for you. I defy you to find a song off the radio that has no structure! If you find one, please let me know.

AABA Format

Unlike my rebellion against the "refrain vs. chorus" terminology distinction, I do believe that there is a clear difference between a verse-chorus format song and the AABA format. The "A" and "B" in this format refer to songs that have two distinct melodic sections, but it's hard to pick out one section that functions as a clear-cut verse or a clear-cut chorus. "Hey Jude" and "Yesterday" are classic examples of these songs. Look up the lyrics to "Hey Jude," and you will see that Paul McCartney's lyrics flow like this:

A
A
B
A
B

All the A sections begin with the phrase "Hey Jude" and they have the same chords and melody. The two B sections share chords and melody as well, but they are different from the A section. If you study this lyric, it's not like the B sections contain the main point or topic sentence of the song and the A sections contain the details. They are distinct bits of info. It's cool to have options like this if your song doesn't fit the verse-chorus format. "Somewhere Over the Rainbow" is another classic example of this format.

One variation of this AABA format is the AAA song. Bette Middler's song "The Rose" is an example of this. This song looks like a poem if you read the lyrics, but if you listen, you'll find that the melody and chord progression reveal it is in the AAA format.

It's worth noting again that there is variability in how different songwriters approach naming song sections. You might think of an AAA song as a Verse Verse Verse song where the verses all have the same tagline. That's fine with me. You might call an AABA song a Verse, Verse, Bridge, Verse song. That feels weird to me, but I can roll with it. I've taught many songs to bandmates over the years and I have yet to hear a protest over how I labeled a song section. The key is that you have to be consistent *within* a song. If you decide to call Verse One the "A" section before your first chorus and then you call the second "A" section Verse Two instead, that would be confusing, especially if it had the same melody and chord progression as your first "A" section.

Other Song Sections and Terms

Musical Interlude/Turnaround

Often, songs will have a bit of space after the end of a chorus before verse two begins. This section is called a "turnaround" or an "interlude." If the chords are different from verse to chorus, typically the band will kick back into the verse chords for a few measures and then verse two will begin. I like this because it gives the listener time to digest what you just sang in your chorus. It also gives the instrumentalists and vocalists a bit of time to reset before moving on to the next verse. Frequently, there is a bit of emotional shift that occurs between verses and choruses, so this turnaround section gives you a second to catch your breath.

Post-Chorus

Taylor Swift's "Shake it Off" is a good example of a song with something you might call a "post-chorus." Again, there's not an international governing body that demands we label song sections in a certain way, so we could simply call the section where she sings "Shake it off" repeatedly after the "chorus proper" an extension of the chorus, but this section of the song has its own distinct feel to me, so I prefer to think of it as a post-chorus. It's also catchy as crap, so you go, Taylor. It's a nifty way for her to drive her point home and establish an earworm.

Beat Drop / Bass Drop / The Drop

If you're into dubstep / electropop music / electronic dance music (EDM), there is another section of the song that can follow the chorus called the "Bass Drop," which I'm pretty sure is intended to assess the integrity of your pelvic floor. This bowel-shaking section makes the subwoofers rattle your entire car and will certainly impress the hotties next to you at the stoplight. All joking aside, the "drop" introduces a sudden change in tempo, instrumentation, volume, chords, or all of the above to create an emotional shift in the song dynamic. Picture a dance floor full of bouncing teenagers. When the strobe light suddenly stops, the laser beams come on and everyone feels compelled to dance in slow motion, you've experienced "the drop." I actually do really enjoy this technique, but I apologize for being too old to extrapolate any further. Maybe listen to some Billie Eilish for examples. Now, get off my lawn!

Tag Lines

This is a nebulous term songwriters use to refer to a repeated lyrical phrase in a song that falls at the end of a verse, a chorus or an A or B section of a song. Often, this is the title of the song. Tom Petty does this at the very end of his song "I Won't Back Down." He simply repeats the lyric, "I won't back down" an extra time at the very end of the song. If you listen to my song "Dead Man in a Dream," you can hear that I used this technique at the very end of the song as well and applied a slight variation in the chord progression and melody just to add some spice. If you're writing in the AABA format, you can think of the tag line as a one-line chorus that happens at the end of each A or B section. The song "To Make You Feel My Love," written by Bob Dylan and covered by Adele and Garth Brooks, demonstrates this.

The Outro

The outro is the very last section of your song. It's basically the opposite of your intro, and it's meant to provide some closure for your listener. There are multiple outro techniques you can use to finish your song with intention.

Simple Instrumental Outro You can simply plunk out the chords of the verse or chorus to kind of ramp down. Often the music will gradually slow in tempo (a *ritardando*, for you music nerds).

Ad-lib Outro If you want to spice up an instrumental outro, simply ad-lib some vocals over the top, maybe some of the key words from your chorus or verse, or some nonsense syllables ("la la la, na na na, ooooh ooooh ooooh," etc.). "Hey Jude" is a classic example of an ad-lib outro.

Layered Outro If you want to get super fancy, you can layer your outro. This is often achieved when the verse and chorus chords of your song are the same and you have one (or multiple) singers sing the verse words, sort of in the background, and the lead singer sings the chorus words, or an ad-lib version of the chorus over the top. "Feel My Love" on my 2010 solo album *Ready* is an example.

Repeat the First Lines of the Song Outro This is one of my favorite techniques when it's used well. Lisa Loeb's song "Stay" is a good example. It's a song about a conflict with a lover. She begins *and* ends the song with the line, "You say I only hear what I want to." In my humble opinion, this is brilliant as it emphasizes the often circular nature of arguments. I used this technique in the Beth Kille

Band song "Wrong Side of Gone," which appears on *Stark Raving Songbird*. I chose to begin and end this song, about a person in an abusive relationship, with the lyrics, "I feel like that old oak tree, stuck in the ground." The intention was to emphasize that even though a person can be strong and know what they need to do, there is a cyclical nature to an abusive relationship that makes it difficult to uproot.

<u>Cliffhanger vs. Resolved Ending</u> While this isn't technically a "type" of outro, it is the very last piece of your song, so it merits some discussion here and nicely demonstrates the concept of composing with clear intention. If your song's intention is to make your listener feel like the story is over, with a happy ending, then consider ending the song on a happy major chord to evoke those feelings. If your intention is to leave your listener with a sense of longing, or a sensation that there will be a sequel to this minimovie, then end on a chord that doesn't have the sense of coming home. Or perhaps you could just cut off a musical phrase abruptly without letting the instruments ring out. I think this can be particularly effective with angsty songs. If you end a happy song on a cliffhanger chord, you'll definitely confuse your listener. If that's your intention, then lovely; just be certain you know what you're going for when you do these things.

Lyric and Chord Sheets

I've put two sample lyric and chord sheets in Appendix A, so you can see how I format them when I'm working with bandmates. I'm meticulous in how I format these for a variety of reasons. First, I want to be efficient in communicating the song format to my bandmates so we all know the structure of the song and which chords occur over which words. Secondly, I use bold type and indentations to create an easy visual for everyone. I always make the chorus indented and all bold to help distinguish it from the verses. If you looked at the sheet of paper from across the room, even if you couldn't read the words, you'd be able to see the shape of the song. I believe this shape gets embedded in our brains as we're rehearsing and makes it easier to memorize. Lastly, if I print these out and give everyone their own copy, we can all take notes of any tweaks we make as we're working through it.

In the Beth Kille Band, my bandmates frequently come up with fresh ideas to tweak chords, add solo sections or other funky stuff. When we come back to our next rehearsal, we can pick up where we left off. I know bands that don't use paper, and that's great if it works for them. But my life is busy and my brain is getting older, so I don't want to waste time trying to remember something that was suggested at a rehearsal that happened two weeks ago. Having this all down on paper and saved in a computer file has also saved my butt on several occasions when I needed to call in a sub for a show when a bandmate went down with an illness.

For those of you accustomed to reading musical score, a

lyric and chord sheet might seem sparse. It works for me, the style of music I play, and the bands I'm in. I am not savvy enough, nor would I want to dictate to my skilled bandmates what to play on their instruments. My lead guitarist can glean the key of the song from a lyric and chord sheet and determine where to embellish with solos and licks. My bassist will know the root notes to build around and the drummer can figure out a beat that fits the song. Most rock musicians use their ears and creativity to build around the bones of a song.

Considering Beats per Measure in Song Structure

Chunks of Four

I've noticed a pattern with some novice writers that can make it difficult for them to move forward in their writing and lock in with other musicians: they take a random approach to the number of beats that each song section occupies. It can be cool to mix up the time signature of your song, but if you're doing it at random or accidentally, it can make you and your song feel disjointed. I've worked with clients in my studio who were inconsistent in how they performed their songs as solo performers, and it created confusion when they hired professional musicians to play on their albums. Sometimes they'd hold a note out for four counts, but then the next time they'd sing it, they'd hold it for five or six counts. This made it very difficult, if not impossible, for the band to follow along.

The vast majority of the songs we've grown up listening to on the radio are in 4/4 time. That means there are four beats to a measure. When you're writing lyrics and creating chord progressions, it may help to keep this in mind. Now remember, I am one hundred percent for creativity here. You can absolutely write in unique time signatures! But if you feel like you're all over the place with your phrasing and can't figure out what's wrong with the groove of your song, you may want to start counting beats and creating some consistency. This has a tendency to make your songs sound more polished. A metronome, an app or computer program that has a drum machine or virtual drummer could help immensely. You don't have to be mechanical and lose your emotional push and pull, but it may help you establish an internal rhythm.

If you play along with your favorite songs from the radio, you'll find that it's exceedingly common for chords to change every four beats and for chord progressions to be built on four-bar phrases. Take "What's Up" by 4 Non Blondes as an example. The entire song is based on the G, Am, C, G chord progression. Each chord is played for four counts and those four chords loop around. Each section of the song (verse, pre-chorus, and chorus) plays that four-chord progression two times through. Linda Perry tricks us into feeling like each section of the song is unique, because of what she does melodically with the lyrics. The band adds in new riffs and instrumentation in the different sections to spice it up too.

Extensions and Contractions

Extending and contracting song sections is a technique that I play with sometimes that helps to keep things fresh. This is a violation of the "Chunks of Four" concept, done with clear intention. For example, compose your first pre-chorus so that it's longer than pre-chorus two. If you've established a pattern in the first pre-chorus that your listener expects, and then you deliberately violate that, it provides a bit of a surprise effect. If you listen to Gin, Chocolate & Bottle Rocket's song "Uphill and into the Wind" carefully, you'll notice that pre-chorus one is just slightly more drawn out than pre-chorus two. It's subtle, but there are four fewer beats before the chorus hits the second time around. Shawndell Marks and I did this purposefully to mix it up when we wrote it.

Way to go! You made it. Hopefully you've got a lot of new tools in your toolbox. If you've got an unfinished song you've been sitting on, I encourage you to pause here and see if you can incorporate some of these concepts. But if you're still stuck, don't fret. We're just getting started! The next chapter explores ways to generate song ideas.

Chapter 5: Song Structure
Too Long, Didn't Read (TLDR) Summary

Having a basic understanding of song structure gives songwriters a foundation upon which to build songs. Structure should not be thought of as rules, but rather as tools for construction. The two basic song formats are verse-chorus variations and AABA.

Song sections in the verse-chorus format are:
- Intro: introduction at the beginning of the song
- Verse: the who, what, where, and when of the song
- Pre-chorus: the section between a verse and a chorus that provides a conduit between the two sections, either melodically or lyrically
- Chorus: the why of the song
- Bridges, Solos, and Breakdowns: these sections provide a departure from previous sections, either by switching up the sound or delivering lyrics that create a new perspective
- Interlude/turnaround: an instrumental section typically between the end of a chorus and beginning of a verse
- Outro: the ending of the song, typically after the final chorus

AABA format describes a song with two distinct melodic sections where there is no clear verse or chorus.

As always, the choices you make for the *structure* of your song should serve the *intention* of your song.

Chapter 5: Song Structure
Assignments

1. Learn a cover tune and study the song's structure. Label each section with titles like "intro," "verse," and "chorus" and see if you can identify any other specific techniques (e.g., alternate chorus, layered outro, tag lines, etc.) discussed in this chapter.
2. Type a lyric and chord sheet for a song you've written using the layout outlined in Appendix A. Be sure to label all sections including the intro, turnarounds (interlude), and outro, if applicable.

CHAPTER 6

INSPIRATION

Long before I wrote stories,
I listened for stories.
Listening for them is
something more acute than
listening to them.
——Eudora Welty,
One Writer's Beginnings

The last chapter tackled song structure to give you a framework for your ideas. The next chapter dives deeper into the specifics of lyric writing tips and techniques, but let's focus now on how to find your song's raw material, keep ideas flowing, and eventually harvest enough content for a complete song. My personal philosophy is that there is no such thing as writer's block. That doesn't mean I haven't had periods of time where I've been less prolific, but I've learned to think of songwriting as a sport and my brain as a muscle. Just like there are naturally gifted athletes, there are also naturally gifted writers. But even a football player with a divinely granted talent can't lay around day in and out and expect to score a touchdown. Similarly, a songwriter with a gift can't just stare at a blank wall all day and expect to be inspired.

This isn't a chapter about waiting for lightning to strike. It's about creating the ideal conditions for lightning (even when it seems there isn't a cloud in the sky) and harnessing its power when it does. If you really, really want to write, you shouldn't wait for divine inspiration. Below are some practices that can whip your songwriter butt into shape, so you can be prepared to play the game.

Write What You Know

When you're looking for inspiration, you don't have to go that far. We are all in the midst of *something* at this moment. So, simply put: write what you know. I have heard this phrase uttered by countless songwriting instructors over the years. Why is this so important? Because authenticity can shine brilliantly. It's much easier to write when you draw on your own personal experience versus trying to write what you think someone else's experience might be. And, frankly, I believe your listeners know when you're handing them a bunch of bunk.

So sit for a moment, turn off your devices, and just think. What is going on in your life? What are you feeling? Who are you ruminating about? What do the people in your life mean to you? How do they make you feel? What are your hopes and dreams? What do you want to teach people? What do you want to learn? What is going on in the world? What is in the headlines that piques your interest?

As the Music Director for Girls Rock Camp Madison, one of my favorite things to do is wander around when the kids are in the midst of the songwriting process and see what their amazing youthful brains are creating. I snuck into one particular band's rehearsal several years ago and the kiddos looked a bit frustrated. When I asked what was up, they told me they just couldn't figure out where to go with their song.

So I inquired, "What is your song about?"

They replied, "It's about a break up."

"Uh, how old are y'all?"

"Nine," "ten," "nine," "nine," "ten."

"And how many of you have gone through a break up?"

Crickets.

So we chatted. I asked them what was going on in their lives. What were they excited about? What was troubling them? We had an amazing and truly insightful conversation about how they all felt like it was hard to just be themselves sometimes. They felt pressure to be perfect, dress just so, or always say the right things, but it was just too much to deal with some days. So we scrapped their breakup song and they started crafting a new song around this idea. The lyrics literally poured out of these kids and in about ten minutes they had rewritten the song, nearly completed it, and it became a camp hit. That song was delivered with such conviction and resonated with so much emotional truth that one of my adult songwriting friends (in her thirties at the time) covered the song at her shows.

Think about how Taylor Swift's career has evolved. The songs she was writing when she was a teenager were filled with teenage love angst that allowed her to connect with millions of young listeners who could relate. As she's grown older, she has adopted a different style and sings about different topics because she's experiencing different things. This isn't Taylor "abandoning her roots." This is her continuing to be true to who she is, as who she is changes and evolves.

The songs I wrote twenty years ago are generally very different in content than the songs I write today, as I'm in a different place than I was back then. That's not to say that everything I wrote back then is dead to me now. It's just different because I have a lot more life experience. So don't be afraid to use your real life as songwriting fodder.

Side note/rant on life experience: if anyone ever tries to tell you someone is "too young" to write a song (or too old), let me loudly say: This is total bull. If you *write what you know*, there is no age restriction on creativity. The perspective of an eight-year-old may be vastly different from that of a thirty-eight-year-old, but it doesn't make it any less real or worthy of expression. We need to encourage writers of *all ages* to pour out their hearts. Aaaand I'm stepping off my soap box. Thank you.

Grasp This Concept: Emotional Truth Does Not Equal Nonfiction

Writing what you know does not mean you can't write fiction, and crafting fiction does not mean you aren't writing your emotional truth. Years ago, one of my songwriting instructors gave our class an assignment to write a song based on a movie scene. I had recently watched the movie *Eternal Sunshine of the Spotless Mind* with Jim Carrey and Kate Winslet. The premise of the movie is that a scientist has discovered a way to erase painful memories and the two main characters decide to erase each other after a heart-wrenching breakup. The message of the movie, in my mind at least, is that if you lose a painful memory, you don't learn from it. So you'll end up making the same mistakes over and over until you learn the lesson you're supposed to have learned from the painful experience. Also, if you erase all the bad memories from your time with a person, you'll lose all the good ones as well.

The movie is brilliantly crafted and shows the process that happens inside Carrey's character's mind as Winslet's character is erased from his memory bank. The memories getting erased are unfolding in reverse chronological order, and of course, as they near the beginning of the relationship, the memories are much more sweet than bitter. In one romantic scene, we see Carrey's character fighting to cling to a lovely recollection. So, while I've never gone through the process of having the memory of someone erased from my brain, I can relate to the desire for it, coupled with the knowledge that painful memories serve a purpose. The message of the movie resonated so deeply with me that it was easy to capture those ideas in the Clear Blue Betty song "Days Like These." Is it fiction? Yes. But is it true? Also yes.

Understand that Emotional Truth Does Not Always Have to Be Poignant

It's true, some of the most memorable songs are ones that make you cry. And, of course, tearjerkers can resonate deeply with our listeners, but there are emotions other than "poignant" worthy of exploration. At a songwriting conference in Nashville years ago, a writer (I wish I could remember who, as I would love to credit him) said something that made the crowd laugh, but was loaded with wisdom. He said, "Live Like You Were Dying" and "Honky-Tonk Badonka Donk" both had emotional truth. They were just different truths.

So please don't cast aside a song idea just because it's not deep, poignant, or designed to cure all human suffering. One of the most requested songs at my live shows provides a good example. I often introduce this song to new crowds as "a song about addiction," frequently explaining that I've been playing music for a long time, and that I've seen some of my musician friends fall prey to the demons of substance abuse. I strike up a syncopated minor chord progression, then launch into these lyrics:

Verse 1

I'm not a victim of any addiction
Of the rock n' roll life
I ain't got no cravings for sugar or candy
I don't need no sweet things to get me by

Pre-chorus 1

But if you're looking to take me down
There's only one thing I can't live without

Chorus

Chapstick
Ch-ch-chapstick
Oh so good on my cracked lips

Oh, oh, no matter strawberry or cool mint
No, no, no, no, no
I don't want to live
Oh, no I don't want to live
A minute without chapstick

Verse 2

You can take my Lexus, it ain't so precious
You can have my diamonds and pearls
Vandalize my mansion with every intention
Of trashing and burning my whole world

Pre-chorus 2

Take my brother, take my lover, too
There ain't no man that does what lip balm can do

Repeat chorus

Bridge

Now I could care less if I ever win the lottery
I only dream of a lifetime supply of Burt's Bees

Repeat chorus

Why do people love the stupidest song I ever wrote so dang much? This truly used to vex me! I think part of it is the element of surprise when I hit the chorus. People like to laugh, and I think it's good for them to know that I don't take myself too seriously. But it's also because you either are, or you know, a chapaholic. Right? It's relatable. It's "truth." It's certainly my truth! So please lift the metaphorical weight off your songwriter shoulders of trying to make every song "The Answer to Everything" and just write a lip balm song from time to time.

Come to Your Senses

Inspiration is literally everywhere. Learning to walk through the world as a songwriter is a skill you can hone, if you work at it. Carry around a notebook or a recording device, or download a recording app to capture sounds and your thoughts. Collect snippets of ideas, and use them to help craft songs when you make time to sit down and further flesh out the idea. I have written songs inspired by license plates, overheard conversations at coffee shops, birds flying overhead, misheard song lyrics, words my son uttered when he was two, book titles, snowflakes, and recurring dreams. I have learned to see life as one big opportunity for inspiration.

So if you're feeling blocked, try to use all your senses and just take in the world around you for a week (or heck, maybe the rest of your life). Ask these questions:

What do I see?
- Billboards
- Newspaper or magazine headlines
- License plates
- Book titles
- Nature (plants, animals, mountains, oceans)
- Friends, family or children

- Strangers
- Buildings
- Highways
- Furniture

What do I hear?
- Overhead conversations in public
- Sounds of nature (wind, birds, a waterfall)
- Family/friends
- Rhythms in the road when driving or in the gas pump when pumping gas

What can I feel? **(Internal and external sensations)**
- Temperature
- Surfaces (soft/hard, rough/smooth)
- Emotions (pleasure/pain, elation/depression, anxiety/stillness)
- Steady/Unbalanced

What can I smell/taste?
- Coffee (That's all I've got.)

Learning to take something tangible that you experience with your senses and turn it into something metaphorical is a technique we'll explore later, but songwriters do this all the time. In the previous chapter, I referenced a lyric I wrote about an oak tree being stuck in the ground and how that mirrored the emotion of the character in the song. Spin your favorite tunes and listen for these metaphors.

Journaling

While this isn't something I've made a regular practice of in my adult life, I know many people find journaling helpful, and I often make time for this in my songwriting workshops. Simply put a pen to paper or sit at your laptop and start writing. Don't stop for five, ten, or fifteen minutes, and write everything and anything that comes to mind. It could be about something in your life that you're trying to process (a loss, a fear, a desire); it could be about a relationship; it could be about an experience; it could be about an addiction to chapstick! Literally, just write whatever. Open the floodgate. Do *not* edit anything. Do *not* judge. Do *not* stop until the timer dings. Even if you just write, "This is dumb. I have nothing to write" for ten minutes, maybe you'll end up writing a song about feeling uninspired! See! Anything can happen.

I also believe strongly that sometimes the best lyrics come when you *stop trying to write lyrics*. It may sound counterintuitive, but remember, the two halves of our brains favor different executive functions. When the analytical left half of our brain kicks in and starts counting syllables and reciting the alphabet to find rhymes, you may disrupt the flow that your right hemisphere prefers and lose touch with the gestalt of the song.

Try Spider Writing

This is a concept I was introduced to many years ago and often pull out as a fun exercise for songwriting workshops. It's similar to free-flow journaling, but is a bit messier and more fun, in my opinion. Take an idea, concept, word, song title that you want to expand upon and put it in the center of your paper with a circle around it. For example, maybe you want to write a song about the beach. So you write "beach" in the center of your page and circle it, like it's the body of a spider. Then you add a spider leg to it and write the first word that comes to mind at the end of the leg, perhaps "sand." Then you lengthen that spider leg beyond "sand" with a word that sand inspires, like "gritty," and then extend the leg past gritty and keep going till that spider leg peters out. Now go back to your center word, "beach," and create a new leg with a different concept, perhaps "seagulls calling," and expand on that leg now. You can have a spider with as many legs you like, all of varying lengths. Tap into your senses. Don't overthink it. Again, we're just brainstorming. Feel free to get goofy. (This can be really fun with a group of people). What often ends up happening is you find cool new words, fresh metaphors, awesome imagery, fun adjectives, and other fresh and fruity stuff to use in your song.

Learn Cover Tunes

Yes, I can hear you cry, "Eek! No! I won't play songs that I haven't written! That's selling out!" Okay, reality check time. When I first started performing, I very reluctantly put cover songs on my set list. I *totally* had the mentality that playing other people's songs wasn't my style. I was an artist. (Please insert here an image of me as an indignant French woman shouting, "*Je suis artiste*!" and you'll have a perfect vision of young Beth.) But learning cover songs can be an incredibly helpful tool. It teaches you how the pros craft songs lyrically, melodically, and chordally. I hosted a showcase called "Sing It Sister" for a decade where I was in a house band that learned songs for six different performers that gave us three songs each to learn. Four times per year for ten years, I arranged charts for the band to prepare for the show. The songs could be originals or cover tunes. So I literally learned over six hundred songs in the process of preparing for these shows. This was an incredible exercise for me in learning how other writers crafted their songs. You do *not* have to learn six hundred cover tunes (go for it if you want), but even if you tackle six, you'll glean some valuable insight.

It's worth inserting a note here on originality. In the immortal words of Steven Page and the song he performed with Barenaked Ladies: "It's All Been Done." If you're worried that you can't write a song because someone else has already written something similar, I get it. You don't want to be a copycat. But while I strongly encourage you to reach for fresh ideas, please don't hold yourself to some impossible standard such as, "Well, everyone sings about love/heartbreak/ loss/blah/blah/blah, so if I can't come up with something new, I shouldn't write." That's just not fair. Not every song you write can be some fresh new invention, and that's okay. Don't let this stop you from creating.

Pick Up a New Instrument

I'm primarily a guitarist on stage, but I dabble in other instruments including piano, mandolin, and bass. Picking up an instrument where I'm a relative novice changes my approach drastically. These four different instruments each have a unique timbre, which can evoke different emotions. There are so many electronic instruments you can play with these days on these newfangled cell phone apps (pardon me while I grab my bifocals so I can see them) that you don't even have to break the bank to purchase a shiny new fender from Guitar Center in order to mess around with sonic inspiration.

Flip Your Flow

I know writers who start with lyrics and think they have to get all the words just right before they pick up their guitar or head to the piano. If that's your style, you may find it liberating or inspiring to flip the direction. Compose a chord progression or come up with a melody using nonsense syllables ("blah blah blah" is my favorite) and then try to plop some words on top of it. We've talked about emotional truth already when it comes to lyrics, but what about the emotional truth of the *music*? The way you play the instruments behind the voice creates the backdrop, just like a scene in a movie creates a mood. Freddy Kruger in a sunny field of flowers just doesn't have the same vibe as a serial killer in a dark forest. So design the scenery and the set with your instruments, and then develop characters and a storyline that fits it. Who knows where it might take you!

My experience with this music-first technique (since I love to start with words) often freaks me out. I might start with a guitar riff, begin babbling over the top and eventually write something and think, "Huh, I have no idea where that came from." And then later, it'll hit me that I'm actually uncovering dark recesses of my psyche that I have failed to acknowledge. It's not always that scary, but you never know what might surface if you stop thinking and just let it flow. Sigmund Freud would be so proud.

Start with a Drum Beat

There are a variety of ways to access computer generated drum beats. I once spent an entire month writing songs to random drum beats generated by Logic ProX's virtual drummers. I just picked a tempo, selected a drummer, and let the beat roll while I riffed on the keyboard, my guitar, or while making up dummy lyrics. I wrote some clunkers, but there were also a few gems.

Do February Album Writing Month (FAWM)

If you haven't heard of February Album Writing Month (FAWM), I strongly encourage you to check it out. Visit the FAWM website and see how writers from all over the world come together on this platform to try to write fourteen songs in twenty-eight days. Think it's impossible? Don't sell yourself short. There are literally thousands of writers on this website. And many of them are looking to collaborate. For example, maybe you'll write lyrics for a tune, but you don't have a melody or music to go with it. Post those lyrics and see if someone else picks them up to collaborate. Or shuffle around the website to find other writers who you like, and see if they're interested in working with you on a tune. It's the coolest thing. Everytime I do this, I get a ton out of it. Usually I start out with a few songs that feel kind of forced and aren't really what I call my "best work," but then something clicks and the songs start flowing. What if you set out to write fourteen songs and only write six? Well, holy moly! You wrote six songs! Right?! You literally have nothing to lose. So push your limits and try it.

Side note: I've heard many new writers express concern that their songs might be "stolen." While I am empathetic to this worry, the likelihood of this happening is exceedingly low. Please don't let this be a barrier to you sharing your art. It doesn't hurt to take some precautions. I do keep records of song drafts on my computer. For example, the first draft would be labeled "Title of My New Song1." Then when I do a rewrite, I'll do a "save as" and call the new version "Title of My New Song2." I often email myself lyric ideas and save Google Doc versions too. I have an app that came preloaded on my iPhone that lets me record and retain melody ideas or rough drafts of tunes. These are all time stamped by the computer or my phone. I figure on the off chance that someday someone steals one of my songs and makes a boatload of royalties, I can dig these up as proof and consult a lawyer. You can register your work through the US Copyright Office if you choose as well. I did that early on in my career but, frankly, I'm lazy about this now. Legally the moment you write it down or record an original work, you own the copyright. Here's the bottom line: create with abandon and don't let the threat of theft keep you from sharing your art with the world.

Lower Your Standards

Something I've learned to embrace wholeheartedly when I'm doing FAWM is this: lower standards. Perfectionism is like songwriter kryptonite. It'll zap your ability to fly. Give yourself permission to suck. I mean it. If you think every song you write needs to live up to the standards of the songs you hear on the radio, that's *totally* unfair for so many reasons. The songs you hear on the radio are typically uber polished with fancy music production, professional musicians on all instruments, vocal pitch correction and effects applied liberally, and some billion-dollar record label pumping cash into a hotshot studio. That's not to say these folks aren't talented. They sure as heck are, but you have no idea where that song started. You also have no idea where the writer of that song started.

When you first begin a songwriting journey, it can be difficult to separate yourself from your creations and to know what is going to appeal to the rest of the world. Here's the thing: it doesn't matter. When you're starting out, every song can feel like a precious child. You should love them with all your heart. This might be a delicate time for you as a new writer, so you should surround yourself with others who see your newborn's beauty. After you've birthed a couple hundred babies, though, it's okay if you forget some of their names. The more you write the less attached you might feel to all the things you've created. That's not necessarily a bad thing. It doesn't mean your heart isn't in it. It just means you've got a new perspective. If you're looking for tunes that have "crowd appeal," you may find it helpful to make basic recordings of your tunes, set them aside for several weeks, and then listen back with a more objective ear.

I heard hit songwriter Craig Wiseman speak at a conference back in the early 2000s. He said he had about three thousand songs in his catalog at that point and thirteen number one hits, which is considered *wildly* successful in the industry. But let's do the math here. Thirteen divided by three thousand = 0.00433333. That means 0.4 percent of his songs have hit number one. This is less than one percent! So if you've written, say, maybe two or three songs or even fifty songs, you probably just need to keep going. You will learn and grow with every song you write. Commercial appeal is not the only reason to compose music. Just sayin'.

Schedule a Co-Write

The adage "two heads are better than one" definitely applies to songwriting. Co-writing is a great way to find inspiration. In fact, if you look up the songwriting credits on songs you know and love, you'll often find the names of more than one writer. Co-writing is an artform in and of itself, though. It requires a lot of trust and can feel a bit like dating. There are some people you'll be compatible with and some whom you won't. It's all good. And open relationships are totally legal in songwriting. You can write with many different people if you choose and not get in trouble. A writer who complements your strengths can be a huge asset. Maybe you're a melody queen, but lyrics don't come easy; pair up with a poetic friend! Or, if you're an instrumentalist who is awesome at jamming and throwing down grooves but need someone to rein you in to create some structure, look no further than your favorite spreadsheet king. There are in-person as well as online creative groups everywhere it seems these days, so find some peers and surround yourself with their inspiration.

Embrace the Theory of Abundance

Mindset is a critical part of finding inspiration. Embracing the theory of abundance helps in all areas of your life and is critical in the creative realm. I wholeheartedly believe that I will never run out of ideas to write about. That doesn't mean I won't tire of writing one day (unlikely, but you never know) but, if I want to write, I know that there are more topics to explore in songwriting than there are hours left in my life.

Practice Makes Prolific

The more I practice my craft, the more natural it becomes. I've been at this for decades and it's definitely easier today than when I started. My brain just works this way now, to the point where I often write songs in my dreams. (I rarely remember them but, trust me, they're all smash hits!) Much like an athlete wouldn't spend her days sitting on the couch eating potato chips to prepare herself for the game, a songwriter shouldn't just sit around and wait for a perfectly crafted song to fall from the sky into her lap. Sure, there are examples of songwriters writing amazing songs in five minutes, but ask any pro writer how many times in their life that has happened, and I guarantee you that is the exception not the rule. Most of them get up every day, grab their instrument of choice and their book of random ideas, and start noodling to see what happens. When we open our minds, our hearts, our senses, and our emotional awareness to what is happening in the world around us, when we invest time in our craft, and we give ourselves permission to be imperfect, we will find we are immersed in a world full of inspiration.

Chapter 6: Inspiration
Too Long, Didn't Read (TLDR) Summary

Finding fodder for your songwriting requires effort, but can be simple at the same time. We explored these concepts for finding inspiration:

- Write what you know.
- Grasp the concept that emotional truth does not equal nonfiction.
- Understand that emotional truth does not always have to be poignant.
- Come to your senses and use sight, hearing, smell, taste, touch.
- Journal or do Spider Writing.
- Learn cover tunes.
- Pick up a new instrument.
- Flip your flow.
- Start with a drum beat.
- Do February Album Writing Month.
- Lower your standards.
- Co-write.
- Embrace the theory of abundance.

Chapter 6: Inspiration
Assignments

1. Set a timer for ten minutes and journal without pausing on a topic that is close to your heart right now. After your timer rings, read your words and see if you can circle a "main idea" or key word/phrase that could serve as a chorus for a song.

2. Go for a walk and bring along a method to record potential song ideas. Remember to use all your senses to find inspiration.

3. If you have written songs before and have a typical approach to composing, try to flip your flow. For example, if you like to write all the words first, start with music. If you like to jam first, start with words.

4. Visit fawm.org to learn more about February Album Writing Month. If it's January or February and the website is "open," sign up.

CHAPTER 7

LYRIC WRITING TIPS
AND TECHNIQUES

In an iconic scene from the film *Music and Lyrics*, the characters played by Drew Barrymore and Hugh Grant debate the importance of words during a co-write session. Barrymore's character, Sophie Fisher, is a lyricist hired to work with a notoriously shallow and floundering pop artist, Alex Fletcher, played by Grant. Fletcher encourages Fisher to just "spit it out," because after all, they're "just lyrics." Fisher counters with an analogy. In her view, melody is like that first physical attraction you feel to a potential new mate that makes you cross the room to learn their name. But lyrics tell their story and make you continue your pursuit. You need to find both attractive for magic to happen.

Legendary record producer Quincy Jones expressed a related sentiment: "Melody is king, and don't you ever forget it. Lyrics appear to be out front, but they're not; they're just an accompanying factor. If they're good, you're really in good shape."

I begin our chapter on lyrics with these quotes for a reason. We are, once again, artificially dissecting the components of a song for convenience. But please do not lose sight of the fact that these words are meant to be accompanied by music.

I have been to numerous song critiques where songwriters hand out written copies of their lyrics, sing their song for their fellow critics, and when the performance ends, everyone directs their attention to the written word on the page. They start micromanaging with feedback such as, "Well, you used the word 'love' twice in the second verse . . . so um . . . maybe replace 'love' with 'infatuation?'"

There's nothing inherently evil with this type of feedback. Maybe it would make the song better, but what about the fact that you would *never* have noticed in a million years that the performer used that word twice if you weren't staring at lyrics on a piece of paper? How many people stream songs with a lyric sheet in front of them? I'm willing to bet it's not that many.

I invite you to look at the tips and techniques in this chapter as additional tools for your toolbox, but please don't get so caught up in them that you lose sight of the fact that *how* you write lyrics is totally dependent on *who* you are, your *individual voice*, and your *goals* as the writer. Please burn this into your psyche before you read another single word of this chapter.

If the critiquers don't know what you're trying to accomplish with your song, they may as well be speaking "wah-wah-wah-wah-wah" like the Peanuts cartoon teacher. It took me a long time to understand this. Your voice is *your voice*. And your lyrics have everything to do with the *intention* of your song. I don't want you to overthink this "intention" concept during the "inspiration" phase, especially in the first steps of your writing journey when you're learning about your unique lyrical style. You might stifle your muse by rigidly defining a goal at the outset. If you have an idea, get it down, and play with it. Then after you've spent some time crafting it, you can retroactively fit it with an intention.

Conversational vs. Poetic Lyrics

Knowing if your lyric style is conversational or poetic is another helpful tool. Your style can certainly be a combination of these, but depending on your genre, you may lean more heavily in one direction than the other. Rock and folk writers traditionally generate songs that lean more heavily on metaphor and poetry. If this is the style you gravitate toward, you may be able to get away with things that wouldn't necessarily roll off the tongue in daily conversation.

If you listen to country music, you'll notice that most country lyrics are quite conversational. The words they use are ones that you could speak to a friend without having them looking at you like you were trying to be the next coming of Shakespeare.

A good example of what I consider a "poetic" song is U2's "Pride." If you look at the lyrics, you'll notice strings of words that probably wouldn't be said in casual conversation. Can you imagine saying the words in the first verse while chatting with your friend Joe at the bus stop? It wouldn't exactly roll off the tongue (and Joe might give you a weird look).

But if you look up the country tune "You're Gonna Miss This" performed by Trace Adkins, you'll find that the song is conversational. In fact the song captures a conversation between a young woman and different people in her life. The writers of these two songs use different styles. Both have merit and beauty.

And don't mistake a conversational style of writing for being banal. There are tons of clever country lyrics. One of my personal favorites is in Carrie Underwood's song "Wasted," where she sings, "For one split second, she almost turned around but that would be like pouring raindrops back into a cloud." Dang it, that's good stuff. Simple, conversational language, but still so artful.

How to Get Away with Lyrical Murder

Something else I've never seen in a songwriting book before is the admission that if you have a killer voice dripping with emotion or you are in a band that makes me want to bang my head / pump my fist / dance my face off, you can likely lower your lyrical standards and get away with it. Adele is a talented songwriter, but take away the voice and you may find some of her lyrics are just average. But when she *sings* them, they take on a new light. If one of your "whys" for writing is that you have a voice that drips with emotion, you may be able to exist on a different plane than the average lyricist. Or maybe you have a band that is the next Rolling Stones and people just wanna groove with you, so you don't have to dig too deep. A song and its performance are all about the emotional impact. Think about Robert Plant. If you're not familiar with the song "Rock n' Roll" by Led Zeppelin, check it out. That song is *all* about the rocking *and* the rolling. Lyrically though, it's nothing special. Robert Plant actually rhymes love with love in the second verse. (Heresy!) But who the flock cares? I listened to this song for twenty-five years before I was forced to learn the lyrics when asked to perform it at a one-off show, and *never* noticed that. And I'm a *huge* word nerd. If you don't at least tap your toe when you hear this song, we need to check for a pulse.

I'm not telling you to intentionally write bad lyrics. (But

hey, maybe that would be fun?) I'm just saying that you can find tons of examples of lyrics that aren't "genius" but that still make you want to sing because they are presented in a way that moves you. We're not writing poetry. We are writing songs.

On the flip side of this, you may be a maestro with words. Maybe your vocabulary is prodigious. (Yes, I just used a fancy word on purpose to sound smart.) But does that mean you have to use that in your songs? Well, that is entirely based on your unique voice as a writer/performer.

My friend Dana Perry has a deep, introspective style of writing that she very capably sings over the top of some impressive Ani DiFranco-esque percussive guitar. She can slam more syllables into one line of a song than I do into entire verses, and she sounds freaking cool doing it. Me, on the other hand, I like to throw in the occasional big word, but I find it challenging to pull that off, both from a vocal perspective and an authenticity stance. The word "transmutating" just doesn't roll off my tongue, but if you look up Dana's tune "All is One," you'll find she makes it work.

Alrighty now. I'm stepping off my soapbox. Time to get down to the nitty gritty. We looked at song structure in chapter 5 and inspiration in chapter 6, and now it's time to craft your masterpiece with all of that beautiful content you've mined and lay it over the top of your solid foundation. Let's geek out on lyric writing techniques!

Impactful Lyric Writing Techniques

Show, Don't Tell

"Show, don't tell" is a classic phrase uttered by many creative writing instructors. But what exactly does it mean? Well, it's, eh-hem, easier for me to *show* than tell you.

Tell: *She was sad.*

Show: *She traced a raindrop down the window. The gray day echoed in her soul.*

Tell: *Her mom came from a long line of alcoholics, but Jenny decided she wouldn't drink like them.*

Show:
Mama had that whisky slur
Like every generation before her
Jenny saw it every night, but she made herself a vow.
She said, "It's killing me the way that bottle rules your life
and I have prayed a thousand times that you would see the light
I can't take no more
but you can rest assured . . .
This is the end of the line.

"Showing" uses action, scenery, strong verbs, conversations, and our senses to convey the concept.

Telling is okay, but it doesn't excite our imaginations in the same way. With showing, we become more deeply invested in the song.

I grew up listening to my mom spinning Dan Fogelberg albums. He was brilliant in so many ways as an artist. His song "Another Auld Lang Syne" is a mini master class on showing and not telling. It's not to say there aren't moments of "telling" in this tune. In fact sometimes you need to get to the point in a song to set the scene, but there are so many lovely images to wrap our mind's eye around. He describes meeting an old lover in a grocery store on Christmas Eve and the conversation that unfolds between them. Take a moment to look up these lyrics. We're going to use this in the next section of this chapter, so it will help to have them handy.

Simile / Metaphor / Extended Metaphor

This Dan Fogelberg song also contains one of the most beautiful and poignant metaphors ever penned. Metaphor uses a quality of one thing to describe something else that is unrelated, but similar. For example, if I say, "She has a heart of gold," I don't literally mean her heart is made out of a precious metal. But you know that gold is valuable, beautiful, rare, and something to cherish just like your friend's character. Metaphors can be used as part of expressions like this, but they are also contained within imagery. In the last verse of Fogelberg's song, right before the delicious saxophone solo, he sings, "the snow turned into rain." I cry just typing that line! What a beautiful metaphor for nostalgia, longing and sadness.

Simile is similar to metaphor, but it throws in the word "like" or "as." I used metaphor and simile in the verse of my tune "Just Wanna Play" about a woman who loves to play her guitar:

She's a runaway train (metaphor)
Skiddin' right off the tracks
Better get out of her way
*'Cause she is swinging that guitar **like** a battle ax*
(simile)

With these lyrics I was trying to paint the image of a woman who just loses herself on stage when she's playing guitar. If you've written a song and want to take it to the next level, look back over your lyrics and see if you're "showing" and not exclusively "telling."

Memorable First Line

One of my favorite techniques is to grab listeners from the get-go with a memorable first line. Sara Barellis demonstrates this beautifully in "Love Song" with the lyrics "Head under water. . . . " Or how about Simon and Garfunkel's "Hello darkness my old friend . . . ." And then of course, we have "Jeremiah was a bullfrog. . . . " Say whaaaaaat??? Keep singing please; I have to know more! This song is proof that sometimes the wackiest things can be the coolest. If you have a killer line buried in a song, you might consider moving it to a more powerful position, like the very beginning. (Read more on this later in the "Punchlines / Power Positioning" section.)

Direction / Plot Advancement

Just like we would feel bored if our favorite show had the characters acting out the same scene every week, it's generally a good idea to think about how each verse of your song moves the plot forward. Don't say the same thing twice just using different words. Each section should give new information or a change of scenery. I've used Trace Adkins' "You're Gonna Miss This" (written by Lee Thomas Miller and Ashley Gorley) previously as an example, but it deftly demonstrates plot advancement. Each section of the song moves the story forward in time, as the main character of the song goes from high school (verse 1) to the early years of her marriage (verse 2) to her life as a mom (bridge).

Repetition

While I just told you, "Don't say the same thing twice," you get to break that rule when it comes to your chorus/hook/title. This kind of repetition allows people to sing along, even the first time they've heard your tune! Making it memorable could also mean they'll want to hear it again. We'll talk more about hook writing in the following chapters.

Punchlines / Power Positioning for Emotional Momentum

I sometimes like to think of writing lyrics as being similar to writing jokes. You don't want to bury your punchlines in the middle of the joke. If you've written a killer lyric, put it somewhere it shines. A perfectly placed pause right after that pithy line allows your listener time to process your brilliance.

In my chapstick song, you can see an example in pre-chorus two of what I consider a "punchline" right before the second chorus.

> Pre-chorus 2
>
> *Take my brother, take my lover too*
> *There ain't no man that does what lip balm can do*

I sing this line with a hint of snarkiness and it tends to elicit a laugh. I deliberately positioned it at the end of the second pre-chorus right before repeating the chorus again because my audience has already been let in on the "secret" that the song is, unexpectedly, not about drugs; it's about chapstick. Chorus one of that song is my first "punchline," so I wanted to raise the stakes a bit and deliver another funny twist before I repeat the chorus.

This type of philosophy doesn't just apply to humorous songs. You can use it with emotionally weighted concepts as well. Crystal Shawanda's song "You Can Let Go" is an amazing example. In this brilliantly crafted song, we meet a young girl learning to ride her bike in verse one. In the first chorus when she sings, "You can let go now, daddy," she's simply telling her dad to let go of the bike. But in verse two, she's older and the scene here is her walking down the aisle on her wedding day. Now the chorus, with the same words, tells her dad to "let go" because she's going to be okay in her new life as a wife. But then the bridge takes us forward in time and her dad is on his deathbed, holding on because he doesn't want to leave his daughter behind. She utters the same words to him in the final chorus: "You can let go now, daddy." Oof. I'm slayed. And, yes, I'm crying again.

Focus on Your Theme / Write to the Title

If you confuse your listener, you might lose them, so it's helpful to figure out what you're trying to say. What is your main message? As we learned in our chapter on song structure, the chorus often contains the title of the song and captures the main point or "topic sentence." Make sure all the lyrics in your song somehow relate to that. Often when I'm writing, I'll start with a scrap of an idea or a phrase, but as the song evolves, I find myself off on a tangent.

Recently, I started writing a song to a heartbroken friend to reassure them that it's possible to heal. I started the lyrics to the verse with vague comforting words, but when I began composing the chorus, I came up with the line: "We're standing in the Emperor's new clothes." Hmmm . . . that felt like an interesting concept to explore for an extended metaphor. I decided to use that as my hook and title. So I went back into the verse and weaved in more imagery that fit with that theme such as "You stitched her to your heart" and "now you're left with these frayed edges of a hole." Keeping your focus on the main theme and writing to the title often requires some rewriting. I get it. Rewrites are painful. But going back with that last layer of polish can take your song to the next level lyrically, if you're willing to put in the work.

Originality

I taught a songwriting club at a local high school in 2009 and 2010. We did a fun exercise one day where I handed the kids a page filled with a list of nouns, adjectives, and verbs. I asked the kids to combine words in ways they'd never seen before, even if it seemed totally off-the-wall. After some quiet time to work on the exercise, we shared our phrases. We had several good laughs, but we also heard some super cool stuff. It's fun to try to say something we've already heard with a lyric we've never heard before. Some of my favorite examples are phrases like in Sting's song "Fields of Gold," where he sings, "*jealous sky.*" Or in Snow Patrol's song "Shut Your Eyes," where Gary Lightbody sings, "*Learn to wear each other well.*" Ooh la la! Seek out your favorite examples in songs and see what you can do with your own fun list of words to put things together in unique ways. I've provided a list in Appendix B that is similar to the one I shared with my students.

Okay to Cliché

I like to think of clichés like seasonings. You can sprinkle them in but, if you overdo it, you might ruin the dish. Clichés are phrases that are overused and have become commonplace in our language. They may have, at one time, been a unique idea, but it's kinda like that song that gets overplayed on the radio: it doesn't have the same impact that it did when it was first introduced. Phrases like "head over heels" or "wrong side of the bed" fall into this category.

If you want to avoid clichés, think about what it is you're actually trying to say and find a new and fresh image. So instead of, "She got up on the wrong side of the bed," you could try something more descriptive like, "She hollered down the steps, 'You better not burn my toast again!,' so I knew to make the coffee extra strong." I find it fun to play with clichés as well. With our same "wrong side of the bed" cliché we could try, "It doesn't matter if it's east, west, north, or south. Every side of the bed is wrong when you don't wanna get out."

Choose Your Vantage Point

Another fun way to play with your songs is to think about adjusting your vantage point. Who is the "singer" within the song? Are you the main character singing from an "I" perspective? This is the classic first-person presentation. You, the singer, are telling us your story. Or are you telling someone else's story, or perhaps speaking to someone else? This is using a second-person perspective where you address someone as "you." Or are you a narrator, using the third-person perspective?

There are advantages to each perspective, so play with them in your songs to see what works best. An example of a first-person song is "Viva la Vida" by Coldplay. When Chris Martin sings, "I used to rule the world," he's telling us about a story he lived through his experiences. Direct address is a powerful first-person approach used in many songs where the singer is speaking directly to another character. Gloria Gaynor's "I Will Survive" is an example.

Second-person perspective often confuses me when it comes to songwriting. It's hard to sing to only the "you" in a song without tossing in an occasional "I." Frankly a lot of songs dance between first- and second-person and that's cool. Alanis Morisettte did this brilliantly in her breakout hit "You Oughta Know." An example of a pure second-person approach is the song "Shut Your Eyes" by Snow Patrol. In the third-person approach, you can be the impartial narrator. "Two Black Cadillacs" sung by Carrie Underwood is a lovely example. Another is Trace Adkins' "You're Gonna Miss This." An advantage of third-person perspective is that you can skip between characters and their inner thoughts without sounding like you have a dissociative personality disorder. When you take yourself out of the song, you can also preach without sounding quite so preachy, whine without sounding whiny, and tell a creepy story without being the creep. You're letting the story and the characters do the dirty work for you. If Carrie Underwood had sung "Two Black Cadillacs" from the first-person, she would sound like a murderer, probably not the image she wants to put forth. Although she did sing about marrying someone without knowing his last name, and then later she smashed his truck with a baseball bat, so who knows.

To Rhyme, or Not to Rhyme, That Is the Question

I'm frequently asked, "Do my songs have to rhyme?" The short answer is, "Heck no!" Remember, there are no rules in songwriting. It's entirely dependent on the intention of your song. However, rhyming does serve a purpose in writing: it makes lyrics memorable. In that way, it can be part of crafting hooks. Employing rhyme makes it easier for both the performer and the listener to remember. Clever rhymes can also be a source of ear candy (especially for word nerds like me). Let's explore different types of rhymes and how they relate to song structure.

Perfect Rhyme
This is the traditional rhyme we learned in grade school. The final vowel and consonant sounds are the same. Examples include cat/hat/bat or green/scene/lean. These rhymes are lovely, but if you limit yourself to only perfect rhymes, your lyrics could sound overly simplistic. This can be a nice choice if your intention is to keep the song sweet and innocent, or if you're singing for kids.

Slant Rhyme

Rhymes that are close-but-not-quite are commonly called slant, near, oblique, or imperfect rhymes. Instead of rhyming "cat" with "bat," you rhyme it with "had." The vowel sound is the same, whereas the end consonant is close in sound but not exactly the same. Slant rhymes open up a slew of additional word options and can go a long way in making your lyrics sound less forced and more creative.

Compound Rhymes

Compound rhymes, also called polysyllabic rhymes (or "multis" in hip-hop) are ambitious rhymes where more than just the end syllable and consonant sound are related. They can be perfect or slant rhymes. Some are created by words that are multisyllabic (e.g. braided/jaded, pedestal/chemical,) but you can also combine words (e.g. high time/my crime). Listen to hip-hop music to find lyricsts who are masters of this kind of rhyme.

Internal Rhyme vs. End Rhyme

Rhymes found at the ends of lyrical phrases are aptly named *end rhymes*. But *internal* rhyme refers to two or more words in the middle of a phrase that rhyme with each other. Here's the chorus of a song I wrote (unreleased) called "Recalibrate" that makes use of internal rhyme:

Time to recalibrate, reevaluate, recalculate all
you know
Realign and redesign, 'cause the future happened
years ago
Recalibrate, reevaluate your equilibrium
Reassess this wicked mess so you can rise up
when the reckoning comes

The end rhymes are "know/ago" and "equilibrium/comes." The internal rhymes are "recalibrate/recalculate/reevaluate" and "reassess/wicked mess."

Trailing Rhyme

Trailing rhymes occur when one member of the rhyme pair has an extra vowel/consonant sound at the end that the other doesn't possess. For example, "believing" and "leave" share the "eev"sound, but believing adds the "ing" at the end. The feel of trailing rhyme is also captured when an extra word is sung at the end of a phrase, but the quality of an end rhyme is still captured in the vocal delivery. For example, when the phrase, "It doesn't feel *right*. I don't want to *fight* anymore," is sung in a way that the word "anymore" doesn't receive much emphasis, the ear hears right/fight as an end rhyme, but it allows the singer to make the phrase feel more conversational and less forced.

Making Rhymes with Invented Words

If you're desperate for a rhyme but come up dry, why not just invent a word? When my friend Shawndell Marks and I wrote the Gin, Chocolate & Bottle Rockets' kids' song "Be Your Own Superhero," we came up short on a rhyme for hero, so we got silly and went with this:

> _Have no fear-oooh_
> _Be your own superhero_

You won't find "fear-ooh" in Merriam-Webster's Dictionary, but it totally works in this song, especially since it's meant to be lighthearted.

Working Hard to Find Rhymes

If you want to take your song to the next level, don't settle for forced rhymes. Work hard to seek out alternative phrases to say exactly what you mean to say. If you're writing in a conversational style and contorting grammar just to get that end rhyme, it can take your listener out of the moment and feel a bit "cringe" (as my twelve-year-old likes to say). There's a game I've played with songwriting students that exemplifies something pro songwriters do in their heads all the time. I call the game "Say It Again." I have students arrange their desks in a circle, write a one-line sentence/lyric at the top of a sheet of lined paper, and tape the page to their desk. They then rotate to a new desk every forty-five seconds and write a new version of their neighbor's sentence below it. They continue to rotate until they arrive back at their original desk, and then we read all the lyrics that were inspired by that original phrase. For example, it might look like this:

1. I can't forget how you hurt me.
2. The pain you caused is stuck in my heart.
3. Your knife is still embedded in my chest.
4. You left me lonely and bleeding.
5. I've never felt so betrayed.
6. You are the dark shadow that hangs over my bed at night.
7. You're the ghost behind my blank stare.

This exercise teaches students that there are limitless ways to express an idea. If you look through this list, I've got seven different potential end rhymes (me, heart, chest, bleeding, betrayed, night, stare) that all communicate something similar. It can be tempting to settle for the first idea that comes to mind, but a little extra thought might bring forth something distinct and powerful.

Rhyming Patterns

Rhyming patterns are notated with letters representing the end rhyme, such as AABB, ABAB, ABCB, or AABCCB. In this method of notation, AABB is a rhyme scheme where lines one and two rhyme with each other (AA) and lines three and four rhyme with each other (BB). In an ABCB song, the second and fourth lines rhyme with each other, but lines one and three don't have rhyme partners. (Don't confuse this notation with our earlier discussion of AABA songs; we're using the same letters here, but now they're representing end rhymes instead of song sections.)

You can choose whichever rhyme scheme suits your song, but typically once you've established a pattern for one section of a song, you'll want to use that same one the next time that song section appears. For example, if your first verse uses an ABCB pattern, you would use that same scheme in verse two.

Switching up the rhyme patterns between sections of your song can be a subtle way to introduce contrast. Here are the lyrics to my song "End of the Line" to show you an example of using a variety of rhyme schemes within a song, but being consistent within song sections.

Verse 1
Daddy had a heavy hand
Just like his father and his father's old man
And it was all Joey knew
But he knew it was wrong

Pre-chorus 1
Joey turned seventeen
One day daddy raised his fist
Joey blocked it with his arm
Said, "Let me tell you this,
I know that's all you know to do
But I'm not like you . . . "

Chorus
"This is the end of the line

I may be one of yours but I am not one of your kind
And I won't make the same mistakes with any child
of mine
This is the end of the line"

Verse 2
Mama had that whisky slur
Like every generation before her
And Jenny saw it every night
But she made herself a vow

Pre-chorus 2
She said, "It's killing me the way
That bottle rules your life
And I have prayed a thousand times
That you would see the light
I can't take no more
But you can rest assured"

Repeat chorus

Bridge
Joey hit the road
Beatin' on his drums in the band
And Jenny's eyes were opened wide
Drinking down the sunsets in foreign lands

Repeat chorus

If we map out the rhyme scheme in each section of this song, we can see the variation from one section to the next but also the consistency within a section.

> Verses one and two: AABC
> Pre-choruses one and two: ABCBDD
> Chorus one, two and three: AAAA
> Bridge: ABCB

Mixing up the rhyme scheme gives each section of this song its own unique identity, but there's also the satisfaction and orderliness of hearing it repeated. This is another way to dance the line between repetition and contrast in songwriting.

A Thesaurus and Rhyming Dictionaries Are Your Friends

Full disclosure: I use rhymezone.com like it's going out of style to come up with rhymes when I'm writing. It also has an amazing thesaurus feature that I've consulted close to ten times in this chapter alone. It's a great way to expand your vocabulary without pulling a brain muscle. If you really like writing the alphabet across the top of your lyric sheets to find every word that rhymes with "bat," (let's see . . . cat, drat, fat, hat . . .) I won't take that away from you. It's great to have that skill set if your internet is down, but I readily admit that computers are smarter than me. Rhymezone even has a "near rhyme" feature. If you think this is cheating, I respectfully disagree.

Singability

Often, subtle word changes make words fall off your tongue more easily. Changing "this" to "the" won't drastically change the meaning of a line, but the elimination of the consonant "s" at the end of the word may make it more singable. I recently wrote the word "harsh" in a song, but realized that there were too many vowel sounds for my face to process, so I just changed it to the word "hard" and it was instantly more singable and didn't change the meaning at all.

When we write songs at Girls and Ladies Rock Camp, we frequently brainstorm lyrics/concepts as a group. We write them all on a big post-it note on the wall and then start playing around with them. When it comes to the concepts and images in the song, I'm all about the collaboration, but when it comes to the nitty gritty specifics of words, I encourage the band to defer to the singer. We all have our unique voices when we speak, just like we have our unique voices when we sing. If you're co-writing and you're not the main singer, you may need to compromise. If we want our singers to shine and be able to deliver songs with conviction, we need to let them use the words and phrasings that fall off their tongues.

Those are all the words I have about words for now. The next chapter explores some of these concepts further as we attach our lyrics to melody. Writing great lyrics takes work. If you want your lyrics to shine, you'll need to embrace rewriting. Walking away for a day or two and coming back can give a fresh perspective. Sometimes our brains solve problems when we stop trying to solve them. Also, it's easy to become overly attached to our "babies" and want to protect them at all costs, but an overprotected child might not grow into a high-functioning adult. Open-mindedness to others' ideas and non-attachment to our own can yield lovely new creations.

Chapter 7: Lyric Writing Tips and Techniques
Too Long, Didn't Read (TLDR) Summary

Writing great lyrics takes effort, but knowing these tips and techniques can help you write lyrics that sing.

Tips

- First and foremost, remember that lyrics are attached to music. You may be able to get away with lyrical murder with a shiny musical package complete with killer vocals and an amazing band.
- Get to know your songwriter voice. Is it conversational or poetic?
- Show, don't tell, your stories.
- Use metaphor and simile.
- Grab your listener with a memorable first line.
- Repetition is good when crafting a hook, but also keep it fresh by advancing your story with each new section of your song.
- Don't bury powerful / memorable / humorous lyrics in your song. Put them in places they can shine, like right before a pause in the song or right before your second chorus.
- Write to the title or your main topic to keep your listener from getting lost.
- Originality is memorable and impactful.
- Clichés are okay, but don't overuse them.
- Explore first-, second-, and third-person vantage points to find what best serves your song.

- Remember, you're not writing a poem, you're writing a song. Your lyrics should be singable.

Rhyming Techniques

Rhymes are not required, but can be a way to make your song memorable. There are an endless number of ways to express a thought, so don't settle for the first rhyme you think of, especially if it sounds forced. Use tools like thesauruses, rhyming dictionaries, etc. There are a variety of rhyme types you can use, including:

- Perfect
- Slant
- Compound/multisyllabic
- Internal
- Trailing

Rhyming Patterns

There are many rhyme patterns to choose from: AABB, ABAB, ABCB and so forth. Mixing up the pattern you use between sections can help create contrast, but it's generally a good idea to use the same rhyme scheme for a specific section each time it occurs (e.g., verse 1 and verse 2 are the same, and/or pre-chorus 1 and pre-chorus 2 are different from the verse but the same as each other).

Chapter 7: Lyric Writing Tips and Techniques Assignments

1. Look up the lyrics to two of your favorite songs, or

use the lyrics for your original tunes and answer these questions for each:

- Are these lyrics conversational, poetic or both?
- What rhyme scheme, if any, is being used?
- If there are rhymes, circle the "perfect" rhymes and underline the "slant" ones. Make note of any internal, compound or trailing rhymes as well.
- Is the song in first-, second- or third-person?

2. Play the "Say It Again" game outlined in the "Working Hard to Find Rhymes" section of this chapter. Take one line from a tune of your own, or choose from one of the phrases below. Write eight different ways you could express the same thought with different words for each of the phrases. Do your best to "show, don't tell."

- I need a change of pace.
- You make me so happy.
- She doesn't care.

3. Use Appendix B to come up with funky combinations of adjectives, nouns, and verbs to create ten unique new expressions. Craft a song around this phrase if desired!

CHAPTER 8

MELODY

Before we dive into the logistics of writing melodies, bear with me while I philosophize on this piece of the songwriting puzzle that comes so naturally to some and is a mighty struggle for others. I have a theory that, in the world of music making, some of us are "emoters" and some of us are "technicians." While I shudder at reducing the world to a binary, I want to explain the extremes of this continuum based on my experience of working with hundreds of musicians over the years. I believe it offers insight on the task of melody writing, both in explaining why it can be a wily beast, and in offering ways to harness both the free-flowing right half and the structured left half of your brain to overcome melody writing struggles.

Emoters and Technicians

When I was going into ninth grade, I taught clarinet lessons to sixth graders who were brand new to their instruments. I remember finding it interesting that some students were very mathematical in their approach to learning. They couldn't necessarily *feel* the beat, but if I gently tapped my foot on top of theirs and told them to articulate a note with each tap in order to play quarter notes, they were able to grasp the concept. They knew exactly where to put their fingers on the instrument when the sheet music directed them to play a D or an F. When they had to play eighth notes, which required dividing the quarter note precisely in half, they approached it like they were solving an equation. They simply divided the quarter note by two. These kids were what I came to think of musical *technicians*.

Other kids just grooved. They knew how "Mary Had a Little Lamb" sounded and, even though they had musical score before their noses, they were actually playing by ear. They could be easily tripped up if you threw a hitch into a well-known melody. For example, introducing a quarter rest (pause) between the words "had a" and "little lamb" would result in a musical misstep, because they weren't *really* reading the notes on the page. They were using a mental construct of how the song sounded to reproduce it. Some of these kiddos needed a little more prompting to attend to the notes written on the page so they didn't become "that kid" who made the loud squawk on their instrument while the rest of the band was silent. These were my *emoters*. I see this in many of the kids who come through Girls Rock Camp. They can't *not* walk in time to the music. On their camp applications, we often read statements like, "I just love to dance and move to the music!" Emoters are the toddlers you see in Tik Tok clips who dance, make up their own words to a tune, and strum a mini inflatable guitar with reckless abandon before they're out of diapers.

I fall hard into the emoter category. As a young clarinetist, I marveled at the technicians in the band. I had to work hard to make sure I was playing the right notes at the right time. Once I figured that part out, I would just kind of use the sheet music as a reference, and I was largely playing pieces from memory or by ear. Sight-reading was a skill I learned, but it was painful. If I heard a piece of music before I played it, I felt much more at ease with my first attempt to perform.

How does this apply to melody writing? I believe when composing melodies, some of us fall more on the *emoter* end and others fall more on the *technician* end of the spectrum. Maybe you're the type of songwriter who doesn't consciously think about the notes you're singing when you compose. You just let them pour out. This is totally acceptable and it's likely your instincts serve you well. But the risk of existing only on this end of the spectrum is that you might end up in a rut, writing the same generic melodies for many of your songs. (I stand beside you guilty as charged). Or perhaps, you're in a phase of your journey where you don't even know where to start with melody writing because you feel like you need someone to write it down with numbers and letters on a page. That is A-OK! Perhaps you're more of a technician. We will talk about ways you can "math" your way out of these tricky situations. Writing impactful melodies is a learnable skill. If you force yourself to be mentally flexible and engage both your emoter *and* your technician, you will be a melody-writing maestro.

Melodic Parameters, Tips, and Techniques

Whether you're the kind of writer who plops melodies on top of your lyrics, or you mold words over melodies, or some combination of the two, making intentional note choices impacts your ability to capture and keep your listener's attention. Let's start with the most basic definition: Melody is, quite simply, the notes you sing when you voice the lyrics. These notes have three basic attributes:

1. Range
2. Duration
3. Dynamics

Let's dive into these concepts.

Melodic Range

If you sit at a piano and find the key that matches the pitch of the highest and lowest note you sing in a song, this shows you the song's melodic range. Someone like Bob Dylan may only span six keys on the piano, while Mariah Carey might belt out a five octave range. Don't worry if you're not Mariah Carey, though; it's possible to be innovative in a limited range.

Here are a couple of specific techniques related to melodic range to consider when crafting your melodies:

Put Your High Notes in the Chorus

Singing higher pitched notes announces to your listener that you're saying something important. Choruses pop if you write the verse in a lower range. The chorus, after all, is typically where you state your "topic sentence" or song title.

Keep in mind, though, the importance of your song's intention. I've written songs where I actually wanted the chorus to feel more intimate than the verses, so I chose to make the chorus more quiet and low in my range than the verses. If you check out Beth Kille Band's "Everything

Beautiful," you'll see what I mean. This is a song I wrote for my son about how life often feels wild, but that he represents "everything beautiful" in a crazy world. I wanted the verses to feel more unhinged and the chorus to feel more like a whisper to a beloved child.

Bump Notes

Sometimes it's fun to put a big interval jump in between two pitches sung in succession. To do this, simply start out a phrase on a lower note and then bump up suddenly to a higher pitch. In Sheryl Crow's tune "If It Makes You Happy" the first two words of the chorus,"If it," are sung on D above middle C and then on the word "makes," she jumps up an octave. Miley Cyrus does this on the verses of "Wrecking Ball" and Ryan Tedder of OneRepublic displays some impressive range on the song "Counting Stars" when he strings out the word "I" in the pre-chorus.

One last note about range: you may find you've got a sweet spot in your vocal range where you've got tons of power and control. This is a nice place to start, but don't be afraid to play around and explore all the facets of your voice. A good vocal coach could be an asset here. If you run an internet search on voice instructors, you're bound to find someone in your neighborhood to help. When looking for a good fit, explain to your potential instructor the genre of music you want to sing. An opera singer uses different techniques than a country singer. Speaking from personal experience, you might be surprised how much there is to learn about vocal cord function, breath support, vowel shaping, and myriad other techniques to improve your vocal health and flexibility. It's true that some singers are born with a gift, but a professional singer has likely had hours of instruction to hone their craft.

Melodic Duration

If you think of pitch as the vertical landscape of your lyrics, duration is the horizontal. It's how much time you spend on the syllable of each word.

Here are some melodic duration ideas to play with in your songs:

Pacing

This is a term used to describe how many syllables you're cramming into a musical measure. Are your lyrics rapid-fire like Eminem? Or are you milking each syllable for all it's worth like an Etta James ballad? Study the songs you love and listen for how the pacing varies from one section to the next. Songs like Norah Jones's "Don't Know Why" have a languid delivery that suits the emotion of the song, as well as her vocal stylings. The pacing of this melody feels relatively consistent from section to section of the song, however, when she sings, "My heart is drenched in wine," each word is given a half note (2 beats) in measure. They feel dragged out compared to the words, "I waited till I saw the sun," which fall faster from her lips. Varying your pacing in lyrical delivery keeps it fresh for your listener. Adele uses this in "Rolling in the Deep" as well. When she sings the verses, the words go by relatively fast. When she gets to the chorus, though, she gives us a double whammy by launching the melody up in her range as well as stretching out the word "all" in the phrase, "We could've had it all."

Point of Entry

"Point of entry" is a term I use to indicate what beat within the measure you start to vocalize. Do you start singing your words on the first beat in the measure (like in the chorus of "We Will Rock You" by Queen)? Or on the second beat (like in the verses in "Sound of Silence" by Simon and Garfunkel)? Or are you mixing it up? I find it very helpful to consider "point of entry" when I compose a first draft melody to a song and get that "Hmm . . . I think I've sung this before" feeling. My go-to melodies come in on beat two, but sometimes I force myself to try a different point of entry. It sounds awkward to me at first because my neural circuits want the familiar, but I overcome that with repetition. Different points of entry can impact the emotional feel of the song as well. For example, entering on the first beat (commonly called the downbeat) can give your song a sense of urgency. Play with this and see how it feels to mix it up.

Sing Like You Speak

One relatively straightforward technique to create melodies from lyrics is to simply sing like you speak. This is a helpful trick for my "technicians" who write words but don't know how to turn them into a song. Here's how it works: read through your song *out loud* and listen to what *syllables* get accented within the words, as well as what *words* get emphasized within your sentences. This can offer insight into a melodic shape. For instance, when I first started writing a song called "Left to Imagination," I didn't have a melody in mind for the chorus lyrics, I just had the words, "Reality is so complicated. It's best we left it to imagination." When exploring ways to sing this phrase, I simply started walking around the room like I was in a dramatic movie scene, repeating it over and over. I found myself putting emphasis on the word "so" in the first sentence. I decided to sing a higher, longer note on the word "so" because I wanted to emphasize it.

You may find the need to occasionally rework

lyrics when using this technique, if you establish a melodic pattern in one section of a song and try to reuse it with new words. I was working with a client in my studio once who was singing a killer melody for his first verse. When he wrote the second verse, he recycled this awesome melody and plopped some new words on top. The lyrics were fabulous, but in trying to preserve the same melody, he ended up singing the word "the" with a lot of emphasis, right before a more impactful word. I can't recall what the word was, but let's just say it was "love." My producer brain kicked in and gently pointed this out. He made a simple tweak to the lyric and was able to put the impactful word on the impactful note, and it communicated the emotion of his song more effectively.

Singing like you speak also helps with intelligibility of lyrics. When you start plopping accents on words and syllables where they don't belong, it causes a mental "Huh?" in your listener's brain. My mom used to jokingly say, "You put the em-PHA-sis on the wrong syl-LAB-ble." It can feel like an undesirable intrusion into your audience's listening flow when singers do this haphazardly. It's a free country, and you can do as you please, but if I'm going to violate the language conventions, I prefer to do this as an intentional technique, which brings us to my next trick.

Don't Sing Like You Speak a.k.a. "Chunking"

You can deliberately violate speaking patterns to create repeatable phrases in your song. I call this "chunking." It's a great technique for crafting a hook (a.k.a. an earworm) to get your audience singing along before the end of the song. Pink's "Sober" is a great example. In the chorus' first line she sings, "I'm safe up high. Nothing can touch me." If you spoke these words out loud, you probably wouldn't pause between the words "safe" and "up," but she does this when she sings it. She repeats the same pattern on the next phrase of the chorus, "No pain inside. You're my protection," when she pauses between the words "pain" and "inside."

When it comes to this melody making device, you may need to get brutal and delete words. Pink could've delivered this in the "natural" shape of a conversation, for example, "I don't feel any pain inside," but she's not speaking; she's singing. And she crafted a clever hook by simplifying the sentiment, "I don't feel any pain inside" to simply, "No pain inside." Remember these are lyrics, not poems or prose.

This chunking technique helps with memorization too. Our brains like information in discrete bits. It's why we put dashes in our social security and phone numbers. When speaking these numbers, we naturally break them up to make them easier to remember and communicate.

Melodic Dynamics

Dynamics refers to the relative loudness of the notes in a composition. For you math nerds, so far we've covered melodic duration on our *x* axis and melodic range on our *y* axis. Dynamics adds that third dimension of the *z* axis. If you read musical score, you're probably familiar with terms such as pianissimo (denoted as *pp*, meaning play very quietly) and fortissimo (*ff*, play very loudly).

When I'm composing, dynamics tend to be an afterthought for me. I don't consciously consider it much until I'm ready to perform, or I'm introducing the song to my band. Although it's an afterthought, it absolutely merits attention when putting the finishing touches on your melody. If I want a certain section of a song to be in-your-face, I'll likely want to sing at a higher volume. But it may demand a tweak in the range in which I chose to sing as well. As a vocalist, I know where my voice loses power (my low range) and where I can really wail (my mid-high range). I've rewritten plenty of melodies or changed the key of a song after an initial first draft when I realized I couldn't sing with a desired dynamic on top of the notes I'd initially selected. If your performance feels too mechanical, it might be worth swinging over to the emoter end of the continuum and exploring dynamics to give your song some nuance.

The Importance of Timbre

In the late nineties, *Saturday Night Live* had two hysterical recurring characters, Marty Culp and Bobbi Mohan-Culp. Will Ferrell and Ana Gasteyer portrayed these prudish music teachers from Altadena Middle School who performed uber-puritanical medleys of modern pop, R&B, or rap songs at various venues. Part of the reason these sketches were so hilarious was that Ferrell and Gasteyer were masters at using their tone of voice for comedic effect. Singing "I like big butts" like an opera singer totally misses the mark, with fabulous comedic outcomes. If you're not looking for comedy, though, you might want to explore your vocal instrument with a good voice coach to harness different styles of singing that best suit the genre of your music.

If you go to a music store and purchase a popular song book, you can learn to play and sing familiar tunes. But simply singing the piece note for note, even if you capture the same melodic range, duration, and dynamics, does not guarantee a stellar performance. A skilled vocalist also knows there are ways to spice up the delivery by varying the quality of the voice as well. Timbre (pronounced "tamber") describes the *quality* of the sound an instrument produces. You may not consider your voice an instrument, but it is. Much like the different instruments in an orchestra elicit different sensations for listeners, the *tone* of your voice can also evoke different emotions. Imagine a ballet dancer dressed as a butterfly trying to convince the audience she's light on her feet to the backing track of a trombone. A flute or piccolo would better fit the bill, right? The timbre of your voice has a huge impact on how your message comes across. If you've got a super powerful set of pipes and love to belt, you may need to reel that in to effectively deliver a sentimental ballad. Conversely, if you're whispery in your delivery, you may need to harness some fire to pull off a punk song. This may be the hardest part to train, but it's one of the most important tools a performer can possess.

I believe this is why there are many successful performers who are not the world's most technically gifted singers. Some performers just make us feel their songs. Mick Jagger wasn't a wildly technical singer, compared to someone like Celine Dion, but he had an unmistakable swagger in his voice. His vocal instrument had a very unique timbre that complemented the Rolling Stone's signature brand of rock, and it moved millions.

Adding the Special Sauce

But wait! There's more! Here are some additional melodic flourishes to consider when composing:

Syllable Extensions
Sometimes it's fun to play around with stretching a word, or a syllable of a word, across multiple notes. Adele's "Easy On Me" has a great example of this when she sings the word "Easy" in the chorus. She stretches the "e" out over several notes to show off her lovely voice. You don't have to embellish that much if your song doesn't require vocal gymnastics. Sometimes just sliding up a note or two within a word can have a cool effect. When Shawndell Marks and I wrote the song "Lean," I remember saying to her that I wanted to add

some zing to the end of the chorus. Being the brilliant writer and vocalist that she is, she suggested we do a stretched out, three-part harmony glide up to higher notes on the word "lean." It proved to be one of the highlights of the song.

Staccato Singing

Staccato notes are short, abruptly delivered notes. Think about how Mick Jagger sings "I can't get no satisfaction." There's a lot of space between those words and it's rad. Billie Eilish does some cool staccato singing in the verses of "Bad Guy." Her halting delivery of the lyric here creates a unique vibe.

Speak-Singing

Adding in a spoken or half-spoken/half-sung part to your song can add an intimate, conversational or sassy feel. Blondie did this in the superhip outro of the song "Rapture." Adam Duritz of Counting Crows slips into this speak-sing in the choruses of "Mr. Jones" on the words "Oh, no, no she's looking at me," creating an almost immediate image for me of the singer and Mr. Jones bantering back and forth while leaning against the bar with a couple beers in their hands. Another favorite speak-sing moment for me is Pink's bridge in the song "Perfect." She alternates between rapping, speaking, and singing about how fruitless it can be to try to please everyone. She ends the bridge with a half-whispered, "Why do I do that?" right before the band kicks back in for an epic ending. For me, that intimately spoken phrase magnifies how personal this song is for her, and I love it.

Nonsense Syllables

There are so many nonsense syllables / non-words to choose from when you're writing. No doubt you're familiar with Michael Jackson's "Hee-hee!" Or his even higher pitched "Ow!" Huey Lewis adds a completely unnecessary, yet totally righteous, "dit-dit-dit-dit" before singing the final chorus of "Heart of Rock n' Roll." The occasional guttural vocalization can be fun like James Brown's iconic "Wah" before he belts out, "I feel good!" So cut loose and experiment with some "woah-woah-woahs" or "la-la-las" when actual words feel bland.

Stutter Singing

A slight variation on nonsense syllables is simply "stuttering" a consonant or vowel sound within a word you sing. A few classic examples of "stutter singing" are the repeated "buh-buh-buh-buh-buh-buh-bad" in George Thoroughgoods' "Bad to the Bone" and The Knack's "M-m-m-m-my Sharona." This technique adds a memorable playfulness.

I'm sure there are plenty of melodic tricks you'll discover, if you keep listening. You'll possibly even create something fun and new, if you dare. Remember there are no rules in songwriting, so challenge yourself to write outside the melody box.

Chapter 8: Melody
Too Long, Didn't Read (TLDR) Summary

Embracing both your intuitive sensibilities and your technical understanding of range, rhythm, and dynamics can help you craft powerful and memorable melodies. Recognize your voice as an instrument and explore how to vary its timbre with a good vocal instructor to take your performances to the next level.

Techniques to try when crafting melodies include:
- Put your highest or sustained notes in the chorus of your song, or in any other section you want to be emphatically heard.
- Play with "bump notes" by creating big interval jumps between two successive notes.
- Vary your pacing from section to section in your songs. For example, if your verses are rapid-fire, make your chorus have longer sustained notes.
- Try different rhythmic "points of entry" into the measure. For example, if you always start singing your phrases on beat two in a measure, mix it up and start your vocalization on beat one.
- Sing like you speak. If you've written lyrics that don't have a melody yet, just speak the lyrics out loud to listen to words and syllables that receive emphasis. Doing this will help you discover a melodic contour to your words. Emphasized words/syllables could be sung on higher notes or stretched out to receive more attention.

- Don't sing like you speak. "Chunking" your words together into hooky melodic bits may violate the natural patterns of language, but it creates memorable motifs.
- Mix it up when it comes to the volume of your performance. Dynamics create an emotional arc for your listener.
- Syllable extensions, staccato singing, speak-singing, nonsense syllables, and stutter singing are other tricks to try.

Chapter 8: Melody
Assignments

1. Look up and listen the lyrics to two of your favorite songs, or use lyrics from your original tunes, and answer these questions for each:
   a. What is the melodic range of the song? Use a keyboard, guitar, or other instrument to determine the lowest and the highest note you sing in the song.
   b. What is the pacing of the lyric? Specifically:
      i. Determine what beat in the measure each phrase begins.
      ii. Are the lyrics in certain sections more rapid-fire than others (perhaps the verse is faster-paced than the chorus)? Or does the tune have similar pacing throughout?
2. Write a one-line chorus for a song. It could be as simple as "I like to play with my voice." Use the melody

crafting techniques outlined in this chapter to create six unique melodies for this one phrase. For example, I could stretch out the word "I" over several beats and different notes. I could chunk up the phrase by inserting rests within the phrase. Just have fun and see how wacky you can get.

CHAPTER 9

MUSIC THEORY FOR SONGWRITERS

In case you skipped the preface of this book, I will repeat: I have no formal music degree. While I'm confident the ideas in this chapter work for songwriters, those of you who have had formal music theory education may find that I approach it differently. If you've never had any formal training, that does *not* have to be a barrier to learning these concepts. If you feel yourself panicking at the word "theory," please take a couple of deep breaths. You've got this. It's not rocket science, but you will have to work to digest these concepts, especially if it's all new to you. Having these tools will expand your capacity to craft songs with intentional emotional impact.

Even if you think you know *nothing*, I promise you'll be amazed by how much you've internalized just by *listening* to music. My students are continually shocked by how much they already know when they realize their ears have trustworthy instincts. Once you learn these tools, it might surprise you to discover how songwriters have been manipulating your senses with this stuff. I'm letting you in on the secret!

It will be easier to wrap your head around these concepts if you can *hear* what I'm talking about, so if you have access to a piano, keyboard, or a guitar, you'll need it throughout this chapter. Download a free piano keyboard app on your smartphone or tablet, if you don't have easy access to an instrument. No excuses! Go get your instrument now. I'll wait.

Okay. You're back. Great! Since this chapter is a bit more complex, I'll highlight the objectives so that you hopefully will feel inspired to see all that you're going to learn! By the end of this chapter, you will:

1. Gain a basic understanding of how chords can be built using notes contained within a major scale.
2. Learn how to use those chords to compose music that has an emotional impact on the listener.
3. Learn techniques to add "ear candy" to your compositions with replacement chords and chord embellishments.
4. Study music you know in order to see how these techniques are applied.
5. Study your own compositions (if applicable) to see if modifications might add impact.

In the Beginning

Bear with me here. I know many of you will already know this first part. But I was teaching saxophone lessons to a doctor once who had never had any musical training, and he came to his first lesson and was struggling, mightily, when it came to reading music. After much head-scratching, I finally figured out that he didn't realize the notes on the scale went in alphabetical order. Here's my point: I was teaching a guy smart enough to graduate from med school a concept that seemed elementary to me, but that was not common sense to him. He had learned that the spaces on the staff spell FACE and that the lines on the treble clef were "Every Good Boy Does Fine." None of that seemed to sing, "A, B, C, D, E, F, G," right? No one is born with this knowledge. It should not be a cause for shame or embarrassment. I'd rather reiterate something you already know than lose you. So, as Julie Andrews sings, "Let's start at the very beginning."

You can reference the keyboard graphic in Figure 1 to help you wrap your head around the concepts introduced throughout this chapter.

FIGURE 1: Keyboard

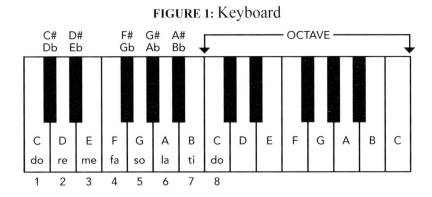

Natural Note Names (The White Keys)

The seven basic notes names of the white keys are: A, B, C, D, E, F, G.

These note names repeat as you play from left to right on the keyboard. If you look at the graphic, you can see the piano key named "C" on the far left. And then, as we climb up the keyboard heading to the right on the white keys, the names go in alphabetical order and the pitches get higher. Once we get to G, we've reached the end of our musical alphabet. So we loop back to A, and then the note names just repeat.

The Octave

Let's discuss the concept of the *octave*. It would be hard to memorize the location of all of our pitches if the musical alphabet started at the letter A and ended at Z! But there's an actual scientific reason that the note names repeat as well. When you strike middle C on a piano, a little hammer strikes a tightly pulled string inside that causes the string to vibrate. The vibration of that string pushes air toward your ear, causing your eardrum to distort, which stimulates your hearing mechanism. The ear sends a signal to your brain and you hear a note ring, one that we have agreed to call "middle C."

These vibrations, or frequencies, are measured in Hertz (Hz). Middle C has a frequency of 262 Hz. If you double that, you get 524 Hz. Middle C sounds like middle C because of the way it stimulates your ear and communicates with your brain. If you double that frequency, your brain perceives that as the same note, but a higher version of it.

Cultural Perception of Music

An octave is a scientifically explainable entity. It's either a doubling or a halving of a frequency. Different cultures over the course of history created different ways to subdivide the tones that occur between octave notes, but octave notes are recognized in most. The standardization of middle C to 262 Hertz is a relatively recent invention in the grand history of music. Before the invention of tools to standardize pitch (e.g., a tuning fork), musicians playing in ensembles would just tune themselves relative to each other.

Our brain perceives certain combinations of frequencies as harmonious and other combinations as dissonant. Some of this can be explained by the mathematical relationship of different frequencies and how that affects the ear. Some of it can be explained by our cultural conditioning to modern music and what has become familiar. Fortunately, we don't have to know the science behind it, but as a songwriter, it helps to understand that we are truly manipulating the brain when we create music. The way we put notes together makes the brain and body react. It's all about creating emotional impact and this impact can be culturally specific.

Intervals

We've covered the white keys, but before we discuss the black keys on our keyboard, we need to learn about intervals. Intervals are the distance between any two notes. If you start on a note and move up the keyboard to the note directly next to it (to the right), you have gone up an interval called a *half-step*. If you go up two notes, you've gone a *whole-step*.

Whole-steps and half-steps use these shortcut symbols:

⊓ = whole-step
∧ = half-step

Let's revisit our keyboard graphic and expand upon it by adding in half-step and whole-step notations below.

FIGURE 2: Keyboard

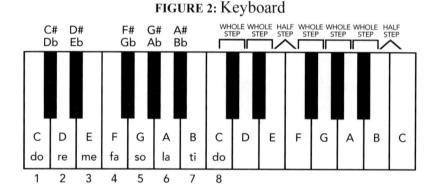

<u>Sharps and Flats (The Black Keys)</u>

Alrighty, back to our note names. We've covered the natural note names on the white keys of our keyboard, but what about those black keys in between? They are special, because they actually get *two* note names. These are referred to as either "sharps" or "flats." If you go to the black key above the A, you call that note A sharp, denoted as A#. You can also call this note B flat (or B♭). When we place # or ♭ before a natural note name, it indicates we need to move a half-step up or down from the natural note to play the appropriate pitch. Here's a summary:

\# = sharp = raise note by ½ step

♭ = flat = lower note by ½ step

So each black key on the piano has two possible note names. Here's a list of notes that are the same sonically, but have two different names:

A# = B♭

C# = D♭

D# = E♭

F# = G♭

G# = A♭

Most often, sharps and flats fall on the black keys of the piano. But . . . (hold on!), if a note has a sharp or a flat symbol and the next half-step is a white key, that's legit! For example, B# is actually also C. And, C♭ is B. Woah! It's helpful to understand this conceptually, even though it's rare to hear someone say "B#" or "C♭."

Scales

The type of scale you play is defined by the pattern of *intervals*. If you put your finger on middle C and walk up one *white* key at a time until you arrive at the octave (high C). You've just played a snippet of a familiar tune: "Do-Re-Mi" from *The Sound of Music*. When you sing "do, re, mi, fa, so, la, ti, do" you're performing a *major scale*. See, you already know some theory! The major scale will be our focus for the rest of the chapter. We will give a brief nod to a couple other types of scales, but now we have our foundation.

When you look at the "do, re, mi, fa, so, la, ti, do" (our major scale) on Figure 2, you'll notice that there are black keys in between some of the words. For example, between "do" and "re," there is a black key and there is also one between "fa" and "so." But between others, there isn't a black key (e.g., between "mi" and "fa" and between "ti" and "do"). If you move from "do" to "re" you've gone up a *whole-step* because there is a black key in between. If you move from "mi" to "fa," you've gone up a *half-step*, because the notes are immediately adjacent to each other on the keyboard.

The pattern of a *major scale* is:

WHOLE-STEP | WHOLE-STEP | HALF-STEP | WHOLE-STEP | WHOLE-STEP | WHOLE-STEP | HALF-STEP

There are different types of scales we can create using different patterns. Another basic scale type is the minor scale.

The pattern of a *minor scale* is:

WHOLE-STEP | HALF-STEP | WHOLE-STEP | WHOLE-STEP | HALF-STEP | WHOLE-STEP | WHOLE-STEP

When you start on a note and play a scale that contains every note (e.g., start on C, move to C#, then hit D, then D#, etc.), you're playing yet another kind of scale, called a *chromatic scale.*

The pattern of a *chromatic scale* is:

HALF-STEP | HALF-STEP | HALF-STEP | HALF-STEP | HALF-STEP | HALF-STEP | HALF-STEP . . . And so on

Why does this matter? Well, now we can use these patterns to build scales in any key we please without memorizing how many sharps or flats are contained within that key.

Let's ignore the minor and chromatic scales for now and only focus on the *major scale*. Head over to your keyboard or pull up your keyboard app. Now, close your eyes and plop your finger down on a random key. Now follow the intervals in this pattern of the *major* scale as outlined above and you will knock out a major scale. For example, if you happened to plop your finger down on the C key on the piano and play only white keys going higher, you would build a C major scale by playing C, D, E, F, G, A, B, C. You skip the black keys because playing them would violate our pattern of a major scale. If you decided to start on the G key, you could build a G major scale by following that same pattern of a major scale and playing G, A, B, C, D, E, F#, G.

If you are a guitar player, you may be thinking, "Um, Beth, there are no black keys on my guitar." True, the guitar is a different creature. Each fret is considered a half-step away from the fret immediately next to it on the same string. So moving up one fret is the equivalent of moving up one key on the keyboard.

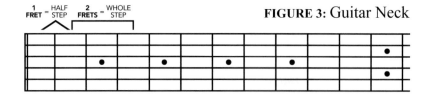

FIGURE 3: Guitar Neck

Grab your guitar (or bass). That big fat open string that is closest to your face, when you're sitting with your guitar on your lap, is generally tuned to an E. If you put your finger down on the first fret and pluck that string, you're playing the note a half-step up from E, which is F. Slide your finger one fret up from F and you get F#. If you wanted to play an E scale on the guitar all on the E string, you'd follow the same pattern of a major scale outlined above by skipping over a fret when a whole-step is required and playing the immediately adjacent fret when the pattern calls for a half-step. Pretty nifty, hey? Note: this is not the way a guitar instructor would teach a guitarist to play a major scale, as it's more efficient to keep your hand positioned over a few frets on the neck of the guitar and play multiple strings. My suggestion to walk up the E string to perform a major scale is strictly for the purpose of understanding the intervals on a stringed instrument with frets.

Why Should I Care What Key I'm In?

As a songwriter who tends to pick up my instrument and start jamming on chords that sound cool, I rarely sit down to write something and say, "Hmm . . . I think I'll write in the key of A today." I usually start humming a melody, pick up my guitar, and start figuring out what chords sound good with my melody. I will explain ways to figure out what chords to play beneath our melodies later, but for the purpose of this exercise, let's say you've composed a little ditty with three chords that all seem to sound lovely together. Maybe you want to add some additional chords, but you're not sure where to go. Finding out what key you're in can help you uncover other chords that can add flare to your tune.

The "key signature," often simply referred to as "the key," is determined by the notes/chords you select for your song. If you're simply playing a scale, it's easy to figure out your key; it's named for the note upon which you begin the scale. If you put your finger on the E note on your piano and walk up that pattern (whole-step, whole-step, half-step, whole-step, whole-step, whole-step, half-step), you will have played the notes E, F#, G#, A, B, C#, D, E. You just played yourself an E major scale. E major is a key signature with three sharps. I'm sure you'll hear that familiar "do, re, mi, fa, so, la, ti, do" pattern, and I bet your ear will tell you if you hit a wrong note. (See, again, how you already know some theory?) Songs built on major scales are pervasive in our culture's school music programs and on the radio.

When you start your composition by playing *chords* that you like, though, it gets trickier to figure out your key. Oftentimes, songwriters don't think hard about this. They just play the chords they know and love and that their ears enjoy. There is absolutely nothing wrong with that! That is exactly how I started. But I eventually got frustrated because I felt limited. Learning a little theory helped me to expand my repertoire. When I figured out the key signature of my song, it helped me find other chords to play that sounded pleasing. Alas, I'm getting ahead of myself. Let me back up and talk about chord building, and then we'll circle back to determining key signatures.

Chords

Chords are built using combinations of notes. "Triads" are chords with three distinct notes in them (tri = three). For example, if you play C, E, and G together on the keyboard, you've played a C major chord. "Major" and "minor" chords are commonly used in songwriting. Let's talk about the difference between them, both sonically and in terms of the intervals between the notes in the chord.

Major Chords

Put your thumb on the E key on the keyboard. Now, count up four half-steps and put your index finger on that key, which is G#. Lastly, count up three half-steps from that G#, and put your ring finger on that key; it should be a B. Congrats! You just played an E major chord. If you're a guitar player, strum an E major chord. It's harder to visualize on guitar because of the overlapping strings, but if you strum an E major, you're voicing the notes E, B, E, G#, B, E from the lowest pitch to the highest. This is also a triad; the only unique notes are E, G# and B, but you have two E and two B notes that are played an octave apart.

Minor Chords

Wait, don't move your hand off that major chord. To build a minor chord, all you have to do is back that index finger down one key on the keyboard to the G, or if you're on the guitar, remove your index finger from the first fret of the G string. Both of these maneuvers have "flatted the third," meaning you lowered the third note in the scale down a half-step. Toggle back and forth between the major and minor chords for a bit. What's the difference to your ears between these chords? Most people would say that a major chord has a "happier" sound and a minor chord sounds "sadder," or more serious.

Chord Notation

You may have noticed that we simply use the capital letter to write a major chord name; we don't have to write "major" after it. A lowercase "m" after the chord name denotes "minor." So "B" means "B major" and "Bm" means "B minor."

Building Chords within Your Key

You'll notice when we built the triad chords above, we played the first, third, and fifth notes of the scale to make the chord. When we build chords, we could build them using three notes right next to each other, but it doesn't sound super musical to our ears. (Play C D E on the keyboard and you'll see what I mean.) But if you put some space in between the notes in the scale by skipping to every other note, it sounds nifty!

Now, look at the keyboard graphic again. Let's say we want to play in the key of C, which keeps us just on the big fat white keys. Listed below are the major and minor chords we can build with these notes using this "leave some space between the notes" approach. Try playing these chords now just for fun!

TABLE 1: Chord Building with Notes Available in the Key of C

Notes in the Chord	Name of the Chord	How the Chord Is Notated
C E G	C major	C
D F A	D minor	Dm
E G B	E minor	Em
F A C	F major	F
G B D	G major	G
A C E	A minor	Am
B D F	B diminished	Bdim or B°

You'll notice this table contains a B diminished chord. Diminished chords are less common, so to simplify our discussion, I'm going to ignore them in this book. Sorry. If you want to explore them, please feel free, but I've written hundreds of songs and have never used a diminished chord, so I'm simplifying.

Roman Numerals Denote Chord Position within a Key

Chords are frequently given a Roman numeral to describe their position within a particular key. An uppercase Roman numeral indicates a major chord and a lowercase Roman numeral indicates a minor chord. Some of the most popular chords in rock, folk, country, pop and hip-hop music are the I (one), ii (two minor), iii (three minor), IV (four), V (five) and vi (six minor). So when you play in the key of C, the chords that are "diatonic" to that key (meaning they're built using the notes in the scale).

TABLE 2: Roman Numeral Notation

How to say the chord name	Roman Numeral Designation	Chord in the Key of C
The one or "the tonic"	I	C
The two minor	ii	Dm
The three minor	iii	Em
The four	IV	F
The five	V	G
The six minor	vi	Am

The chart below outlines some chords available to you in guitar and keyboard "friendly" keys. Of course, you can play in any key signature you like! In Appendix C, you'll find a complete list. When I'm teaching, however, I like to start with the ones in the chart because beginner guitarists can play most of these without having to use barre chords (which are hard to play until you've built up hand strength). I will explain this chart in detail below, but familiarize yourself with the layout before we proceed.

TABLE 3: Chords Built on Major Scale Notes in Guitar and Keyboard-Friendly Keys

Roman Numeral	I ("one")*	ii ("2 minor")	iii ("3 minor)	IV ("four)	V ("five")	vi ("6 minor")
Function	stable	transitional	stable	transitional	unstable	stable
*The key is always named after the I chord	A	Bm	C#m	D	E	F#m
	C	Dm	Em	F	G	Am
	D	Em	F#m	G	A	Bm
	G	Am	Bm	C	D	Em

I recently taught a one-hour songwriting crash course to three different high school history classes where I introduced the concepts of major scales, building chords and then naming the chords with Roman numerals. We wrote the Roman numerals on a white board and I asked a kid who didn't play any instruments to randomly circle three of the six Roman numerals. We built a song using the three chords he selected and the song sounded perfectly musical. How did a kid with no musical training pick three chords that worked? Because any six chords that *share a row* in Table 3 are the chords that songwriters use *ad nauseam* to write the songs you've been listening to your whole life. So you can mix and match them to your heart's content. Go ahead, pick a key from the chart above (say the key of A) and follow across the boxes, that means you can write a song using any of these chords: A, Bm, C#m, D, E and F#m. Play any of these chords together and they will sound like they belong together. Tons of songs have been written on guitar using G, C, D because they're relatively easy, open chords for guitarists to play. But they also sound rad. The reason? Because they're all in the key of G. Just look across the row from G and, lo and behold, you'll see that G, C and D are the I, IV and IV chords. Congrats. You've just learned the secret handshake.

Chord Function

The "position" of a chord within the key will help determine its "function." Notice the word function in Table 3 on the far left column, second box down. This means certain chords will have a certain impact on the listener as you play the song. Some chords will feel stable or "restful" to the ear. For example, the I (one) chord and the vi (six minor) chord will often be the first chord played in a song, the first chord in a chorus, or the chord at the very end, because these chords give the listener a sense of stability. The V (five) chord often makes the listener feel "tension" or instability. Kind of like, "Don't hang out on that chord too long, you're making me nervous."

Speaking in terms of *function*, a commonly used chord progression is:

stable---->transitional----->unstable----->stable

OR

stable---> transitional---->stable----->unstable ------>stable
(or some variation of this)

Try this out if you want to mess with your listener's minds: play a C, F, G progression a few times. This I, IV, V progression is super common. You can hear it in songs like "La Bamba" and "Twist and Shout." This "stable," "transitional," to "unstable" progression really sets the listener up to want to hear the "restful" I (one) chord after that "unstable" V (five) chord to resolve the progression. I dare you to try ending a song like this on the V chord (G). Do it and then just walk off stage without even saying goodbye. Everyone will scream, "No! Get back here and finish that song! Don't leave me hanging on that unstable chord!" Well, okay, maybe not, but they will all wonder if you've lost it. Our ears have been trained by popular music over the past several decades to want that resolution. We use that expectation to our advantage to create an emotional impact. If you want your song to create the sensation that all is resolved at the end, wrap it up with that I chord. If you want to create tension, and leave your listener hanging, end on an unstable (V) or a transitional (ii or IV) chord. Listen to "Radio" by Beth Kille Band for an example of a song that ends unresolved. I did that intentionally just to mess with you. Sorry, not sorry.

I've Written Chords, Now How Do I Figure Out What Key I'm In?

As mentioned previously, when I sit down to write, I rarely set out to write in a specific key. I usually just start strumming, and I play what sounds nice to my ears. I'm not too proud to admit that I used the chart above for *years* before I was able to internalize it. I would write down my chord names, look at the table and say, "Huh, well, I'm playing D, Bm, A, and G. Looks like I'm in the key of D!" I was learning this in the midst of working full time as a physical therapist, commuting forty minutes each way, trying to maintain a household, gigging, writing, working out, caring for my dog, hanging out with friends, and more. I wasn't a full-time music student that used this information all day, every day. So don't beat yourself up if you want to use a cheat sheet to make your life easier.

I recently used this chart at Ladies Rock Camp during a music theory class. The campers shared the chords they had chosen for the songs they began composing with their bands. Of the eight students (representing members of four different bands) in my breakout session, only one of them had any music theory background. Yet three of the four bands had composed songs that all fit nicely within one of the key signatures on our nifty chart above. One band used the chords C, Am, F, and G (they were in C), another used G, Em, and D (they were in G).

There was one band that wrote a song with G, C, D, and E. One of the members, with no prompting from me, said something like, "I love these chords, but that E sounds kinda wonky when we play it." We referenced our chart, figured out that they were playing in the key of G (G was the I chord, C was the IV chord, and D was the V chord) and that E was not "contained" within the key, hence the reason it sounded funky to their ears. But they loved the sonic effect of it. Their song was about spring emerging, and that E chord made it feel like the song was blooming! It fit the intention of their song, so there was no need to say, "Well, that E chord isn't on the chart, so you can't use it." Remember, there are no rules in songwriting. This chart should never constrain your writing or make you doubt your ear.

If you're trying to learn a song you know from the radio (without looking up a lyric and chord sheet), if you determine the first chord of the song, the first chord of the chorus, or the last chord of the song, that will often tell you the key you're playing in, hence what other chords might be in the tune based on that key. I just did this with the song "Hey, Soul Sister" by Train. I was able to figure out that the first chord was E. I simply guessed that was the I (one) chord. I know what the IV, V, and vi chords in that key are: A, B, and C#m, respectively. I also know those I, IV, V, and vi chords occupy many pop songs. And guess what? When I used my ear and tried out those four chords, I had the whole song figured out in a couple of minutes. Boom!

If the song begins or ends on a minor chord, you're likely looking at the vi minor chord. For example, if the song begins and ends on Em, you could conceptualize this as being in the key of G, since Em is the vi chord in that key. Technically, you could say you're playing in Em, *but the key of Em has all the same chords available to you as the key of G.* So I say po-tay-to/po-tah-to. The vi minor chord is referred to as the "relative minor" chord of the I chord. If you recall, the vi and the I chord have two overlapping notes in their triads. The G chord has G, B, and D while an Em has E, G, and B. Both share the notes G and B. Both are considered "stable" chords, so they're related, like cousins who share some of the same DNA. So if you want to have a heated debate about whether you're playing in the key of G or Em, that's cool by me. But at the end of the day, it doesn't make a big difference in the family of chords you're likely to hear in a pop song or the chords you'll want to play when you're composing.

The Circle of Fifths is a diagram some of you may be familiar with that serves a number of functions for composers. For our purpose in this chapter, though, it offers a quick method to find the relative minor of any major key. The major key names are listed in the outer circle and its relative minor key is listed adjacent to it in the inner circle. So if you need to make a mental flip from thinking about your major key to thinking of its relative minor instead, this might serve as a handy reference. If this confuses you, don't fret. I don't personally use this, but it's a handy reference for readers who may have learned this at some point in their musical training.

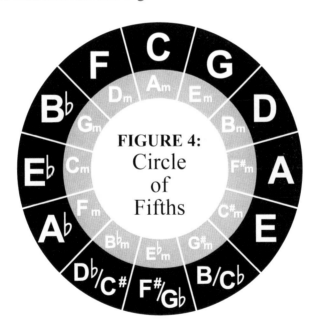

FIGURE 4:
Circle
of
Fifths

If I Write a Melody First, How Do I Find My Chords?

One of the most common statements I hear from emerging songwriters is, "I've written a song that I love to sing, but I have no idea how to figure out what chords to play." Now that we've discussed the major scale, chord building, and key signatures, we have an excellent platform upon which to explore this slice of the songwriting pie.

Let's say I have a singer-songwriter in my studio, we'll call her Bess Kill-Knee, who comes to me and sings words to a lovely melody, but has no accompaniment yet. To help dear Bess, I will sit at the piano and plunk out the notes she sings. I may even write the names of the notes above each word, so I can see a pattern. Let's pretend this is our lyric and I've written the *note names* (not the chord names) above the syllables of each word:

Verse 1
G G G G   F E
I real-ly want to learn
E   E   E   D   C
How to play the chords
C C   C   D C
To the songs I sing
G G   G   G F E A   E
It would mean everything to me

(Clearly, Bess has a smash hit on her hands.) The first thing I notice is that the first verse has a lot of G, E, and C notes.

Bess occasionally dances over a D, but doesn't seem to hang out there for long. I also notice that she isn't singing any sharps or flats. Take a look at our chart. The key of C doesn't have any of those pesky sharps or flats. I happen to know the C major chord is composed of C, E, and G, so I'm going to play that chord in verse one and see how it feels. I can dance around with the other chords in the key of C that my handy chart offers (C, Dm, Em, F, G, and Am) while Bess sings her song. I will use my ears to see how it flows and discover what works best to help her capture the desired emotional tone.

Prosody is a fancy word that means matching the mood of your music to the mood of your lyrics. If I decide I want the song to sound lighter, I might start on a C. If I want it to sound darker, I might use Am instead of that C. Functionally, they're both "stable" chords (Table 3). You'll see they are inner/outer circle buddies on our Circle of Fifths (Figure 4). Remember, since both are stable chords in the key of C, they can be used interchangeably based on the backdrop you want for your melody.

I have yet to do this exercise with a singer and *not* find them singing in a consistent key. It's remarkable to me how much we have all internalized singing and playing within a key. But, of course, we don't want to forget to think outside the box.

Expanding Your Chord Vocabulary Beyond I, IV, V

I've mentioned several times in this chapter that the I, IV, and V chords are very common, but if you want to expand beyond that, here are some techniques to use:

Replacement Chords

Let's say you're composing a song on the piano. You decided that A, C#, and E (an A major chord), D, F#, and A (D major chord) and E, G#, and B (E major chord) seem like a nice combination. But you've played these same three chords over and over, and now you're sick of them and want to expand.

First off, check out Table 3 again and tell me, in what key do you think you're playing? Spoiler alert: you're playing in the key of A. The A, D, and E are the I, IV, and V chords. What other chords are listed on the chart that you could try in your song? Well, you could simply pick anything else in that key of A and they'd sound lovely. Bm, C#m, and F#m are all good friends. If you've already written a melody, you don't even have to change it, you can just swap out your chords with others that have a similar "function." For example, in the key of A, both A (the I chord) and F#m (the vi chord) are "stable." So you could swap out some of your A chords for the F#m, still sing your same melody, and it'll work! You could also swap out that D (IV) chord with the Bm (ii) since they both function as a transitional chord in the key of A. This, again, is because these "cousin" chords share two out of three notes. The Bm chord is B, D, and F# while the D chord is D, F#, and A. They coexist on the D and F#. Similarly, an A chord is made up of the A, C#, and E notes, while F#m is comprised of F#, A, and C#. These two chords share the C# and A notes.

Chord Embellishments

Sometimes those chords you know and love can be dressed up to give them a bit more pizazz. Here are some tricks:

- Sus chords While this may sound like your chords are being suspicious, "sus" actually stands for "suspended." Sus chords are created by removing the "third" of the chord (meaning the third note in the scale) and replacing it with something else. If you recall, the third is the part of the chord that determines whether you're playing a major or a minor chord. If you flat the third, a major chord becomes a minor. If you take out the third and replace it, you create a sus chord. There are two sus chords:
    - Sus2 chords This sus chord "suspends" (i.e., does not play) the third and replaces it with the second of the chord. An A *major* chord contains A, C#, and E. Our Asus2 chord has the A and E, just like the A major, but it replaces C# with B.
    - Sus4 chords Yep, you guessed it. Now, instead of using the second note of the scale, we're suspending that third and using the fourth. So Asus4 is composed of A, *D*, and E. (If you happen to have a piano, try playing A, Asus2, and Asus4 and see if you can hear something

reminiscent of the intro of Tom Petty's "Free Falling.")

- <u>add9 chords</u> add9 chords are secretly related to sus2 chords. Let me explain. There are eight notes in a scale. The first and the eighth note in the scale are octaves of each other. So the ninth note in a scale is actually an octave higher than the second note. You with me so far? If you were playing a Csus2 chord, you would add the second note in the scale, which is D, immediately next to the C note. So on our keyboard, a Csus2 chord would be C D G. The Cadd9 chord plays a regular ol' C chord, but adds that D an octave higher. Cadd9 chords are quite common and easily executed on guitar. They have a slightly richer sound (in my opinion) than a plain old C chord.

- <u>7th chords</u> 7th (seventh) chords are a way to embellish major or minor chords by adding the 7th note in the scale. It's beyond the scope of this book, but know that there are a wide variety of 7th chords available (minor 7th, major 7th, dominant 7th, etc.) that can spice up your song, and add tension or sonic variety. Jazz and blues artists frequently make use of these chords in their compositions.

Power Chords

Power chords are frequently used by rock guitarists. These chords are so punk that they throw away the third, and they don't even replace it! Sometimes these are noted with a five after the name of the chord. For example, A5 would indicate playing only the first and the fifth of the A chord: the A and E notes. These chords have a somewhat ambiguous feel to them when played on an acoustic guitar or piano, since they are neither major nor minor.

Non-diatonic Chords (Ear Candy and "Lift" Effects)

We briefly touched on this concept earlier, but let's revisit the term *diatonic*. A "diatonic" chord is one that is "contained within the key." For our purposes, that means the chord is built using the major scale notes of the key we're in. Using a *non*-diatonic chord can add some interesting "ear candy" into your arrangement by adding notes outside of the key you are in.

One simple technique is to change a major chord to its minor version or vice versa using Table 3. A common example is converting the ii (2 minor) into a II (2 major). Patsy Cline's "She's Got You" does this in the B section of the song. This section starts on the IV chord with the words "I've got your memory / or, has it got me," but then we hear the surprise II chord on the "I really don't know . . . ." It adds a dramatic element and amplifies the emotion in this section.

Adele does this in "Rolling in the Deep" immediately

before the chorus when she sings, "I can't help feeling." Sara Bareillis also employs this in the second chorus of "She Used to Be Mine" on the words "Growing stronger each day." Take a listen to these tunes and hear the "lift" effect this has on these portions of the songs.

Putting Roman Numerals to Use

As a fledgling songwriter, I was issued an assignment to learn all the chords to a song I loved. The next task was to figure out the key of the song, and assign Roman numerals to each chord. I remember rolling my eyes and thinking, "What a pain in the butt!" Looking back, though, I can see it's a useful skill. Understanding the Roman numeral system helps in many ways. With repetition, you will begin to internalize the information in Table 3, quickly identify what key you're in, know what chords are available, and know how to manipulate them when composing.

I often speak in Roman numerals when communicating with my bandmates. I am primarily an acoustic guitar player and I love to use a capo on my guitar to use different voicings of chords. A capo is a clamp that is placed on the neck of the guitar over the strings, which effectively shortens the strings, thus making the instrument sound higher. If a song I'm learning requires me to use a lot of barre chords (chords that require my index finger to press down all six strings at the same time), I can adjust that by putting on the capo and using open chord fingerings. This gives my hand a break from the strain of barre chords. Generally, a bassist and lead guitarist do not use capo. So when I'm playing a song with my capo on the fifth fret of my guitar, and my fingers tell my brain I'm playing a C shaped chord, an F shaped chord, and an Am shaped chord, those are *not* the actual chords I'm playing. My capo on the fifth fret has actually placed me in the key of F. I frequently communicate with my bandmates in Roman numeral language, so I don't have to transpose in my head. For example, I'd say, "I'm playing a I, vi, IV progression; let's end the song on the vi," and they know how to follow along.

Another application of Roman numerals is a charting system for studio musicians called the Nashville Number System. This system makes exclusive use of Roman numerals to communicate chord changes in a song. Songwriters who are not themselves performers, or perhaps want a different singer to represent a song, will hire studio musicians and vocalists to perform their work. Using the Roman numerals allows the studio musicians and the singers to quickly transpose, so they can experiment playing the song in different keys. This allows the vocalist to perform in their ideal vocal range. It also gives the professional instrumentalists license to embellish with their own rhythms and riffs, instead of being constrained to a musical score which specifies each note they should play. I've written songs with male voices in mind and hired musicians to record them. They used the Nashville Number System to transpose my song into a key that was most comfortable for the male vocalist.

Phew! You made it! Congrats on persevering through to the end of this chapter. Be sure to give yourself grace when learning these concepts. With time, effort, and repetition, these ideas will solidify, and you will expand your songwriting bag of tricks. I bet you realized, though, that you know more than you thought. Trust your ears and your heart above all.

Chapter 9: Music Theory for Songwriters
Too Long, Didn't Read (TLDR) Summary

Grasping the basics of music theory expands your understanding of how scales are used to build chords and chords are used to build songs. Here's a review of the basics covered in this chapter:

- The white keys on a piano are A, B, C, D, E, F, G.
- The black keys have two names each: A sharp (A#) = B flat (B♭), C# = D♭, D# = E♭, F# = G♭, G# = A♭.
- An interval is the distance between two notes.
- Adjacent notes are a half-step away from each other. Two half-steps equals a whole-step.
- A major scale (do, re, mi, fa, so, la, ti, do) always follows this interval pattern: whole-step|whole-step|half-step|whole-step|whole-step|whole-step|half-step.
- A minor scale always follows this interval pattern: whole-step|half-step|whole-step|whole-step|half-step|whole-step|whole-step.
- Chords can be built off the notes contained within the scale of your key signature.
- Two basic chord types are in major (happy) or minor (dark). The first and fifth notes are the same in both chords. The third note determines whether you're playing a major or minor chord, thus changing the feeling of the chord.
- The key signature of your song is determined by the

note (or chord) that feels like the central anchor point around which all other chords and the melody dance. It's frequently the first chord of the song, the first chord of the chorus, or the last chord of the song.

- Roman numerals are used to designate the position of a chord within the key signature. The basic chords available to you when playing in a major key signature are the I (one) chord, ii (two minor) chord, iii (three minor) chord, IV (four) chord, V (five) chord, and vi (six minor) chord.

- The I, iii, and vi chords have a "stable" feel to our ears, the ii and IV chords feel "transitional" and the V chord feels "unstable," making us want to hear the song resolve back to a "stable" chord.

- We can manipulate our listener's experience by consciously attending to a chord's function and where we place it in our song. For example, ending on an unstable chord makes a song feel unresolved.

- If you have a song with a melody but no accompaniment, mapping out the pitches you sing can help you uncover your key, hence what chords are available to play.

- If you have a song with only two or three chords and want to expand, determining your key signature, and using Table 3 to determine what chords are available in your key, will help you find replacement chords for your overused ones.

- You can make interesting versions of basic chords with embellishments such as sus2, sus4, add9, and 7ths.

- Composing with non-diatonic chords (those not found within the key signature) can add sonic freshness to your tunes.

Remember, trust your ear. You know more than you think.

Chapter 9: Music Theory for Songwriters Assignments

1. Analyze the chord progression of a song you've written or a cover song (feel free to Google the lyrics and chord progression) and assign the Roman numeral to each chord in the song. What "function" does each chord serve?
2. Take a song you've written or are working on, and see if you can introduce some "replacement" chords for the ones you currently have. You can do this either by completely replacing the chords *or* by changing to the replacement chord immediately after you play the original chord. (For example, if you have a C chord in your song for four beats, play C for two beats, and Am for two beats instead). Make a basic recording of each version and listen. What impact does this have on your tune?

CHAPTER 10

ADDITIONAL COMPOSING CONCEPTS

Before we wrap up part 2, I'd like to share a few more composition concepts to help you pull together the ideas covered so far and write powerful tunes.

Writing Hooks

A songwriter crafts a hook to reel in a listener, just like you might cast a line with a juicy worm to catch a fish. With the right lure, you can land a casual listener in your songwriter net, although, in this case, I encourage a catch and release instead of filet and fry. There is no single tried-and-true technique to create a hook. I briefly introduced one in the lyrics chapter, with the concept of "chunking," but not all hooks are rhythmic, lyrical phrases. Here are some other angles to consider:

Impactful Words

If you're writing a novel or a short story, the hook might be the memorable introduction, that dark, intriguing character, or the cliffhanger chapter endings that keep the reader turning pages. Sometimes the hook is a memorable opening line, but the hook can also be the killer chorus that provides a catharsis for the tension built in the verse. Elle King's "Exs and Ohs" is an example of a clever hook that delivers the punch we're craving after she's listed the string of lovers she's abandoned in her verses. It's a clever play on the "XOXO" we might scribble at the end of a love letter.

King's hook is also the title of her song. This is a common practice. If you're interested in pitching songs to publishers, a good title can get you in the door. I wrote a song with my friend Connie Mims called "Homeless In My Hometown" that caught the attention of a small handful of publishers because they were intrigued by the name. It was unique, but not too weird, and it hinted at a topic many people understand: feeling like a stranger in a place you once belonged. Simply stating the title of a song before performing it might be enough to pique the audience's attention. If I think I have a clever title, I frequently introduce the song with a quick sentence like: "This is a song about contradictions called, 'Not That I Don't.'"

Babble Singing

You can develop hooks with a lyrics-first approach, but it can also be fun to start by singing simple, repeated nonsense syllables that give you a certain emotional vibe, then craft lyrics over that. If you write a melody and it gets stuck in your head, it's likely it will have the same effect on your listener. Repeat that melody and listen closely for its sentiment. Does it make you feel light and airy? Does it make you feel sad? Motivated? Ticked off? Whatever it is, harness that emotion and find words that match. It's likely you've got something rolling around in your subconscious. You can start with "dummy" or "placeholder" words until you uncover the perfect phrase. It's rumored that Paul McCartney started the song "Yesterday" with the words "Scrambled eggs, oh, my darling you've got lovely legs." Whether or not that's true, the words "Yesterday, all my troubles seemed so far away" convey more emotional depth to match that beautiful melody.

Bookending

Bookending is a specific technique songwriters use where they put the hook (or title) at the beginning and the end of the chorus. King's "Exs and Ohs" does this. My song "End of the Line" does this as well. It's different from simply repeating one phrase over and over in the chorus, in that there are other words between the repeated phrase. Here's my chorus:

> *This is the end of the line*
> *I may be one of yours but I am not one of your kind*
> *And I won't make the same mistakes with any child of mine*
> *This is the end of the line*

It's a song about two kids who descend from generations of physical and substance abuse who are strong enough to stand up to their parents and say, "No more!" They refuse to hand down dysfunctional traditions. I didn't repeat the title because I ran out of things to say; I repeated it to bring the message home.

Instrumental Hooks

Name That Tune was a game show that challenged contestants to beat their competitors to the button and name a song after a short instrumental snippet was played. These instantly recognizable melodies, which earned big bucks for the folks on these game shows, are often crafted by instrumentalists, not the vocalist. Think about the opening guitar lick in AC/DC's "You Shook Me All Night Long." Any fan of the band will know within the first three notes what song is coming. It's become what's called a "signature lick" in the industry. Signature licks are musical earworms crafted by an instrumentalist. Stevie Wonder's keyboard riff in "Superstition" falls into this category too. Everyone jumps up to shake what their mama gave them when that groove plays. The percussive sounds coming from a plastic cup created a hook for "When I'm Gone" from *Pitch Perfect.* You don't have to play a complicated passage to create a musical hook. The simple "stomp, stomp, clap" of Queen's "We Will Rock You" is simple, but effective.

"Secret" Hooks

Often a skilled instrumentalist will capture a small piece of a vocal melody hook and incorporate it into an opening lick or a solo to reinforce the hook. Listen to

Taylor Swift's "Should've Said No." The song opens with a banjo player capturing a portion of the chorus melody. This lick gets passed off to the fiddle player once the band kicks in. By the time Swift hits that chorus, you've heard the melody of "Should've Said No," without even knowing that the musicians have been secretly burning it into your gray matter. So sly! I accidentally did this in the Gin, Chocolate & Bottle Rockets song, "This House." I played a stupidly simple, repeated two-note guitar melody in the intro, reminiscent of a doorbell. I unconsciously turned that instrumental hook into the melody of the chorus. I was crafty without even trying!

Names, Numbers, Places

Along the lines of "secret hooks" are song elements that are just so simple that you can't help but remember them. People love hearing songs that use a person's name ("Roxanne," "Jack & Diane"), a city or state name ("Sweet Home Alabama," "Walking in Memphis"), or that spell something ("R-E-S-P-E-C-T"). Using numbers ("Summer of '69") or counting ("1234" by Feist) can also create an instant connection.

Call and Response / Echoes

Call and response or echoed phrases give your audience a chance to sing along. Harry Belafonte's "Banana Boat Song" is a great example, with the repeated phrase, "Daylight come and we wan' go home."

The King of Soul himself, Sam Cooke, does this in "Bring It On Home," with the backup singer leading the response by simply repeating Cooke's "Yeah" at the end of the chorus. If you're an artist who primarily performs originals and don't have a large following of audience members intimate with your tunes, these simple techniques can give them an instant sense of belonging.

Dance Moves

Before you freak out and think you have to learn complicated choreography, let me explain what I mean by "dance moves." Simply inviting the audience to raise their hands above their heads and clap can be a simple maneuver that brings them into the moment. Simple snaps, fist pumps, or stomps work, too. You could come up with your own version of "Y.M.C.A.," writing a song with other letters that can be spelled overhead. When Gin, Chocolate & Bottle Rockets performs "Be Your Own Superhero," we invite the audience to strike superhero poses at the end of each chorus. Simple synchronized movements like these create a playful sense of oneness.

Creating Contrast

Hooks are often built using repetition, but listeners might grow bored if you overdo it. You want both a repetitive and impactful component to make them feel cozy, but then some freshness to keep them intrigued. Monotonous music is fine if your objective is to be meditative, but if you want to prevent people from falling asleep on their barstool, you can do this by creating contrast. Here are some suggestions:

Mix Up Your Groove

A simple way to mix it up is to change up the groove or strumming pattern from one section of the song to another. For example, play an arpeggiated guitar or piano part in the verses and then chunk out chords in your chorus. Kelly Clarkson's "Behind These Hazel Eyes" takes this approach, with the guitarist plucking individual eighth notes in the verses and then breaking into an overdriven guitar strum with a distortion effect on the pre-choruses and choruses. Using a more staccato style in one section and changing to legato works too. If you are a folk songwriter who is always strumming the same pattern on your guitar, listen to genres with different groove patterns like reggae or heavy metal. There are endless combinations of rhythms you can create for your backing tracks. Get freaky and see what happens!

Pauses/Rests

Inserting rests, or pregnant pauses, can startle the audience, in a good way. A musician friend, Jimmy Voegeli, dropped a Zen quote at a songwriter meeting years ago that stuck with me: "It's the space between the bars that cages the tiger." Jimmy is a skilled blues keyboardist, vocalist, and songwriter. While he is capable of playing rapid-fire passages, sometimes it's the pauses in his music that create the wow factor. If you listen to my song "Idlewild River" you'll hear a quick pause after the first chorus that is intended to gain attention before the band really kicks it up a notch in verse two. There is another abrupt stop after a loud solo section before the quiet third verse. When these stops and restarts are executed skillfully, listeners take notice.

Chord Progression Variety

It helps to pay attention to the rhythmic pattern you create with chord changes. For example, are you always changing chords every four beats? If you want to create contrast, keep that pattern in your verses, but try to mix it up and change every two beats in the chorus. Remember those replacement chords in the music theory chapter? They come in handy for this type of contrast. Perhaps you've composed a song with four counts on each chord in this progression: G, C, G, D. Maybe you're doing this throughout the entire song and it feels monotonous. If you don't want to change the melody you're singing, but want to freshen up the chords, you could use some replacement chords to spice up the chorus by changing chords every two beats. So instead of four counts each on G, C, G, D you could change chords every two beats with G, Em, C, Am, G, Em, D, D. Try it out and see how it generates momentum without creating the need for a vocal melody overhaul.

Another way to vary your chord progression without

using a wide variety of chords is to simply change the order of the delivery of your chords from one section to the next. If your verses are G, C, D, G, try making your chorus C, D, G, C. This works best when composing the chords first and then layering the melody over the top. If you've already composed a melody, and then decide to switch up the chord progression, you may need to adjust the notes you sing to be harmonious with the chords you're playing.

Playing with the Band

If you're lucky enough to have bandmates, it can help to think of contrast/variety as it pertains to the parts everyone in the band is playing and how you layer the different instruments throughout the song. Listen carefully to songs you know. Study what instruments come and go from the song section by section and how the level of complexity might change throughout the song. You'll likely discover some surprises like: "Hey, there's a keyboard part that comes in the third chorus that wasn't in any other choruses!" Or: "Interesting that there's no bass guitar in verse one." Or perhaps: "I never noticed that the guitar player was just strumming whole-notes in verse one, but was going nuts in verse two." Sometimes musicians can be a little too in love with their playing, noodling on a song from the first downbeat to the final cutoff. But a break from time to time can create some nice sonic variety.

Time Signature or Tempo Changes

Creating contrast with tempo and time signature changes offers a slick way to grab your listener. Adele's song "Rumour Has It" includes a stylistic change as well as a dramatic tempo slowdown in the bridge before the song kicks back into its driving beat for the final chorus. In my song "Big Bright Beautiful World," I switched from 4/4 (standard rock) time to 3/4 time in the bridge to shake things up. Our brains tend to want to lock in on a stable rhythm, so sometimes it can feel awkward to execute these changes, but with repetition, it will come to feel more natural. When performed skillfully, the listener is drawn in by the novelty.

Key Changes

A key change can add some special sauce to your song. My cowriting friend Erik Kjelland and I used this technique in the last chorus of our Kerosene Kites tune, "All About It." We shifted the last chorus of the song up a whole step. Dolly Parton does this in her song "Coat of Many Colors," in the third verse when she sings, "So with patches on my britches . . . . " Listen to these tunes and hear how the songs take an emotional step up when the key change occurs.

The Truncated Second Chorus

Truncating your second chorus is a fun technique that creates contrast by violating an established expectation. If you listen to James Taylor's "You've Got a Friend," you'll notice that the first chorus ends with him singing the title. But the second chorus skips that tagline and jumps right into the bridge. When I was writing and performing with my band Clear Blue Betty we decided to merge the end of the second chorus and the beginning of the bridge in our song "Back to You."

In the first chorus, I sing:

Time keeps slipping through our hands
Your journey didn't take the path you planned
I see you going in circles trying to tidy up your
past
But it all comes back to you

The second chorus is almost exactly the same except we jump straight into the bridge using the last word of the chorus as the first line in the bridge. Chorus two ends with:

But it all comes back to . . .

Bridge:
You have to realize all the subtle ways you
sabotage yourself . . .

You can utilize countless methods to pleasantly surprise your listeners with contrast. Don't confine yourself to this list.

Before we close, I have a few words of caution. Overanalysis can stifle creativity. My hope is that the tricks and tools I've shared in part 2 will give you fresh perspective, inspiration, motivation, and even a sense of relief in knowing that you have pages to reference when you get stuck. My fear is that you will overthink the process and accidentally suppress your muse. In the preface, I briefly wrote about right and left brain thinking. Be sure to give your right brain ample space to run, chase butterflies, get distracted by shiny things, and admire the sunset. Seek inspiration in these dalliances. But don't forget to use the left half of your brain to gently corral and organize your right brain's "big ideas" into a unique and beautiful piece of art for the world to behold.

Chapter 10: Additional Composing Concepts
Too Long, Didn't Read (TLDR) Summary

This chapter explored these concepts:

Hooks

A hook can be anything that reels your listener into your song-boat. Here are ways to write hooks:

- Craft impactful lyrics, such as a killer opening line or a chorus that delivers a clever catharsis after the verse builds tension.
- Babble sing nonsense words / syllables to find a melody that sticks in your head, then figure out the emotional tone of that melody and write words to match.
- Bookend the title of the song in your chorus.
- Compose an instrumental hook or "riff" with guitar, violin, keyboard, percussion, etc. that makes the song unique and identifiable.
- Develop a "secret hook" by using an instrument (keys, guitar, etc.) to mirror and reinforce a melodic hook the vocalist delivers.
- Use numbers, count, or add specific names of people/places.
- Turn your spectators to participants through call and response, echoes, or "dance moves" like claps, snaps, stomps, poses, etc.

Contrast

We often use repetition to create hooks, but variety/contrast keeps our audience engaged. Here are ways to create contrast:

- Mix up your instrumental rhythms.
- Introduce pauses/rests.
- Vary your chord progressions from one section of the song to the next.
- If you play with a band, have instrumentalists layer their parts in different ways through the song, so that not every instrument plays start to finish without a break.
- Experiment with time signature, tempo, or key changes.
- Truncate your second chorus before the bridge to violate expectations.

There is a balance between running wild without focus and becoming stymied from overthinking. Learn to dance the line.

Chapter 10: Additional Composing Concepts Assignments

1. Pick two cover songs that you consider catchy. What type of "hooks" do these songs use? List all the hooks you can identify, even if they are not ones that were explained in this chapter.
2. Write a song and deliberately employ a hook-writing technique.
3. Pick two cover songs you know and enjoy. How do these songs use contrast? Identify instrumental, melodic, rhythmic contrast, or other techniques.
4. Compose a song and deliberately use the concept of contrast. Explain what techniques you applied and why you chose them.

PART THREE

Part 1 investigated motivations for songwriting and discussed ways to create fertile soil for your muse to thrive. Part 2 explored tips, tricks, and tools for crafting songs. Part 3 introduces some inspiring characters who quieted their demons and overcame barriers to reach their goals. It also presents a compass and some navigational tools for guidance on your lifelong creative journey.

In case no one's told you this lately: you rock.

CHAPTER 11

INSPIRING TALES

I've had the good fortune to work with hundreds of performers and songwriters of all experience levels over the years. My personal mission is to inspire people to use their voices and express their creativity. Ironically, I find that *I* am often the one who is inspired by those who have walked beside me on their artistic journey. I'd like to introduce you to a few of the souls who have touched me and the important lessons they have taught.

Mandi's Story: Breaking Down Walls in Safe Spaces

As the Music Director of Girls and Ladies Rock Camp Madison since 2010, I've seen many campers experience stage fright. "Overcoming performance anxiety" is frequently cited as a reason people choose to come to camp, *especially* Ladies Rock Camp (LRC). The kiddos at Girls Rock Camp certainly report feeling nervous, but the beauty of being young and inexperienced is that no one, including your psyche, expects you to be large and in charge. As we age, we often internalize the narrative that we must be the expert. Especially if we're doing something in front of a crowd. It's okay if we're not perfectly polished in our youth, but as a grown-up, the bar shifts. The fear of failure and rejection from a judgemental crowd can feel overwhelming, and it can build a wall between us and our desire to share our voice.

I met Mandi at a performance in the spring of 2014. Three

years later, she decided to attend LRC. Despite being outgoing and hilarious, Mandi suffered from terrible stage fright. Signing up for camp to learn drums allowed her to conveniently hide behind the cymbals while on stage. During the weekend of camp, she mastered her drum part in three days and even worked up the courage to perform a hysterical monologue during her band's song, voicing the part of an extremely picky and entitled restaurant patron. Her fellow campers, LRC staff, and the crowd went wild for it. I think something subtly shifted for her with that experience, and she became one of our LRC "repeat customers." A few weeks before her third camp, she messaged me to ask if I would play guitar while she sang "Grandpa" by The Judds at the Sunday night showcase. I enthusiastically replied, "Yes!" knowing that this was a major step for her. In a Facebook post, she wrote, "I just took a huge leap of faith—I committed myself to singing at the next Ladies Rock Camp. I have terrible stage fright, but for me, there's no safer place than LRC to work on overcoming it."

We strategized beforehand to help her get in the right headspace. I made a simple recording, with just me on guitar, so she could get the feel for performing that way (instead of practicing with a karaoke track). When it came time to rehearse at camp, even with a small, loving group of her peers, she was terrified. She had a hard time catching her breath and was visibly shaky. She was concerned about how she would fare at the showcase, but we all encouraged her and kept the faith.

When it was her turn to perform the night of the show, she walked on stage with wide eyes and wobbly knees. I strummed the chords of the intro. She took a breath and tried to sing. At first, her voice was so shaky, it was almost inaudible. The crowd, sensing her need for support, cheered her on. She kept breathing. She pushed through and she got stronger with every word. By the end, she was *nailing* it, singing with confidence and pure passion. At the song's cut off, the audience went wild. If you can believe it, I cried. Even a stoic friend of mine in attendance admitted to getting choked up. It was one of the bravest things I've ever witnessed on stage.

The moral of the story is this: you can overcome your greatest fears. Mandi demonstrated this in such an inspiring way. She started with baby steps. She sought support. She prepared. She tested the waters, surrounded by loving and supportive people. And then, she went for it. She looked her fear in the face and said, "Yeah, I see you! But you're not the boss of me!" In an after-camp Facebook post, she wrote, "Wow, another Ladies Rock Camp under my belt! More than anything, I want to take a moment to thank everyone at LRC with whom I shared this weekend, your support and encouragement is never taken for granted. With each camp, you're helping me break down this very large wall I've built around myself. For that, there'll never be enough words to express just how thankful I am. Much love to you all." I hope Mandi's story inspires you to break down your own walls.

Jackie's Story: It's Never Too Late

I met Jackie in the winter of 2013 when she was referred to me by a mutual friend for songwriting lessons. Prior to our meeting, she had recorded a handful of instrumental piano albums of "oldies" tunes with her dear friend, Jay, a talented local producer, musician, and teacher. When Jay died by suicide in August of 2012, Jackie was devastated. She was at a loss about what to do with her grief. So, to process and heal, she turned to songwriting.

Despite being an accomplished pianist and author, she hadn't put words and music together before then. She and I met regularly over the course of several weeks and composed enough songs for a record. Jackie didn't aspire to be a performer, so she hired various local musicians to help with the project. She recorded her tunes with our mutual friend, Billy, at the studio where she and Jay had worked together. The album was released later that year. By the way, did I mention that Jackie was seventy-four years young at that time? And she was just getting started.

That project opened a floodgate. She continued to write songs with various collaborators over the years and released three additional albums of original tunes. She turned the story of her friendship with Jay and the music he inspired into a cabaret-style musical theater piece, with the mission of suicide prevention and awareness. The musical debuted in 2019 to a packed house, receiving rave reviews. When the 2020 reprise performance was thwarted by the pandemic, she turned the play into a movie. All this transpired in her so-called "retirement" years.

If you're flogging yourself for having quit piano lessons as a kid, or failing to pursue that degree in music, I've been there. Done that. But it's time for some perspective. There are countless choices we make in a lifetime. Looking back and wishing you had taken a different path is natural, but all you can do from here forward is work to make decisions that take you in the direction of the life you want. Jackie turned tragedy into art, and it has touched so many lives. If you wish you had started younger, try a trick out of Jackie's playbook.

John's Story: Leave a Legacy

In 2014, Beth Kille Band had a chance to play a large festival in Madison. I received a friendly email from a gentleman named John a few days after the show who had become a new fan at that event. We struck up an exchange on music matters. I learned that he was a guitarist who had played in a cover band years ago and was now dabbling in writing his own tunes. He mustered the courage one day to send me some rough recordings. I instantly felt a pull to help him bring these tunes to life. His guitar playing was great, his voice was reminiscent of Lou Reed, and his songs were unflinchingly raw.

I invited him to my studio to do demo recordings with a few of my kindhearted and talented musician friends who frequented my studio for session work. They too saw the potential in his tunes and encouraged him. Despite this, John battled self-doubt. He worried that his songs were too depressing or that they weren't "rock n' roll" enough. He didn't like the sound of his own voice. He tried to convince me that he would write the songs, play the guitar, and have other people sing on the album. But I wouldn't have it. I told him that these were *his* stories to tell. After repeated reassurance that he had it in him to make this happen, we began the process of recording. Then he went dark for almost a year.

When we reconnected, he explained that he had been in a

funk and just couldn't bear to pursue the project with all his demons in tow. We talked it through, and I offered to connect him with my dear friend and vocal coach, Dana Perry. After a year of working with Dana and plugging away in the recording studio, we captured his tunes in an album-ready format. I saw him at one of my shows a couple days after we'd finished the recording. He looked at me with the sincerest eyes that night and quietly stated, "I think I finally found my voice." I remember a sense of peace emanating from him, as if he'd finally quieted his inner critics.

We had arranged for him to be the "Honorary Dude" at my upcoming "Sing It Sister" event, where he would perform a couple of his songs with the house band accompanying him. He failed to show for the rehearsal, which was extremely out of character. That evening one of John's colleagues reached out to tell me that John had not shown up for work that day and to ask if I had heard from him. Concerned, I contacted the police station in his hometown to do a wellness check. They called me after getting into his apartment to let me know they found him. There were no signs of foul play, nor was there a suicide note. They later determined that he died of an apparent heart attack, at fifty-three. Two nights later, to honor him, we played his recorded voice and guitar with the house band accompanying him. His daughters sat in the audience and wept as his voice and guitar sang out a tune called "Wish" that enumerated all his tender hopes for their lives.

With the help of my friend Chris Franczek, I finished the process of mixing and mastering the album and we "released" it at his funeral. Looking back, it's surreal that I felt such an urge to help him see this album through to fruition. He tried to back out so many times. I could have let him, but something told me to stick with it. I'm glad I listened to the voice in my head and that he found the strength to fight past his insecurities. His daughters now have a piece of his musical legacy. If they need to hear the sound of his voice, they can. Not all children can say that about a parent who is lost so unexpectedly.

Here's the take-home message: you never know when your number's up. If you have something to say, say it while you still can. If you have gifts to share, don't let them die with you. John overcame the deepest self-doubt, and in the process he created something beautiful and found his voice before his time was up.

I could fill another entire book with stories of those who have enriched my life with their courage and tenacity. In the next chapter, I'll share tools you can use to work through your barriers to chart a path forward toward your own inspiring story.

Chapter 11: Inspiring Tales
Too Long, Didn't Read (TLDR) Summary

Mandi's, Jackie's, and John's stories illustrate how we can overcome our fears and cast aside myths about being "too old" to achieve our goals. Each of these people faced barriers but prevailed with hard work, courage, and support from friends.

Chapter 11: Inspiring Tales
Assignments

1. Write down three life lessons you learned from Mandi's, Jackie's, and John's stories.
2. Explain how these lessons can inspire you to keep going on your songwriting journey.

CHAPTER 12

THE THRIVING SONGWRITER

Congrats on making it to the last chapter! Here are some final tools to help you foster a healthy mindset and resilience in the face of struggles. I don't just want you to exist as a songwriter; I want you to thrive. I sincerely hope that these strategies will support you in prioritizing your health, so that your creativity can flourish.

Creativity as Your Compass

We all have different roles in our lives and different values that inform our decision-making in those areas. For example, if you value the environment, you choose to recycle. If you value your health, you choose to eat your veggies. Living with a "purpose mindset" empowers us because it links our actions to our convictions. Christine B. Whelan, dubbed "The Happy Professor" because of her work in the School of Human Ecology at the University of Wisconsin–Madison, helps students understand how having clarity on our values brings contentment. I took an online course with Dr. Whelan where she defined purpose as "using your *strengths* to live in line with your *values* to positively *impact* the lives of others."

In chapter 4, I emphasized the importance of exploring your personal "whys" for songwriting and it's worth revisiting at this point in our adventure. If you've made it this far in the book, I'm going to go out on a limb and assume that one of your *values* is creative self-expression. I'm also willing to bet that your *strengths* align with songwriting. Whether it be the ability to produce melodies, generate lyric ideas, compose chord progressions, or elicit an emotional reaction from a crowd, you possess a certain set of gifts that makes you special and unique. Chapter 1 explored the *impact* of art and how it builds community and brings healing. If we use the template from Professor Whelan above, we can pull this all together in a songwriter purpose statement:

> *I use my **strengths** as a songwriter in alignment with my **value** of creative self-expression to **impact** the lives of others through connection and healing.*

Feel free to tweak this to suit your specific situation, but having clarity about your purpose is like holding a compass. When you clearly identify creativity as a "true north," it makes it easier to know which direction to turn whenever there is a fork in the road. Should you sit on the couch and binge-watch TV seven nights per week? Or should you join that new songwriter's group that meets the first Wednesday of every month? Should you numb out with just one more glass of wine and doomscroll to ignore the grief you're feeling? Or should you journal about it and write lyrics for a song that might help someone else process *their* grief too? Should you let the wounded inner child that was bullied for being a "freak" prevent you from sharing your voice? Or should you sign up for that open mic?

While this compass points us in the right direction, the next step is, well, taking the steps. This can be easier said than done when the road is strewn with potholes and roadblocks. So let's focus next on recognizing and overcoming barriers.

Recognizing and Overcoming Obstacles

According to psychologists Matthew McKay, John P. Forsyth, and Georg H. Eifert in their book, *Your Life on Purpose,* barriers to following our values fall into three main categories: behavioral, cognitive and emotional.[1]

Behavioral barriers are resource-based deficits like time, money, knowledge, or skills. Realistic goal setting is a way to take baby steps toward overcoming these behavioral obstacles. By reading this book and practicing its lessons, you've already taken steps to overcome knowledge-based and skill-based barriers. High five! What other behavioral barriers might you identify? Maybe you want to learn some basic recording techniques, so you can remember the melodies of your new tunes. Maybe you want to sign up for guitar lessons. What about doing weekly YouTube tutorials to become a more confident singer? Or you could reach out to that friend who has been asking you to co-write. Perhaps you hire a sitter, so you can get out of the house next week to do a few songs at an open mic. Each time we identify a behavioral barrier, we are empowered to choose a small goal that pushes us toward the next mile marker.

One of the biggest self-sabotage moves you can make is setting the bar impossibly high. If we feel paralyzed at the foot of the mountain because the summit is above the clouds, it can help to only focus on the first few steps. On the flipside, we might reach the peak and then turn around and ask, "Okay, what next?"

Hollywood presents a faulty notion that once we've reached the mountaintop, we've "arrived," and that's the end of the story. If our focus is solely on checking goals off of a list, we might question why we don't experience that fairytale ending after we reach them. If we keep our purpose in mind, though, we know the summit was just part of our ongoing journey. This is why a purpose mindset *and* goal setting go hand in hand in the thriving songwriter's life.

While our behavioral barriers might be easy to enumerate, *emotional* and *cognitive barriers* may be harder to identify. And they seem to pop out of nowhere some days even after we thought we'd left them behind. Throughout human evolution, survival of the fittest demanded we react to threats in our environment, but when we perceive threats everywhere, our fears take over. *Emotional barriers* are feelings of fear, anxiety, anger, or sadness that elicit maladaptive fight, flight, or fawn (a.k.a. freeze) responses. *Cognitive barriers* are our negative thoughts and self-talk. These are those monsters that like to follow us around and shout things like: "Who are you kidding? You'll never be as good as so-and-so." Or: "Don't put yourself out there, people will laugh at you, and you'll be all alone." Oof. Yeah, I hear them too.

Stephen Hayes, the psychologist who pioneered Acceptance and Commitment Therapy (ACT), developed a valuable metaphor for working with these emotional and cognitive barriers. Imagine yourself following your compass, driving happily down the road in a big yellow school bus. You're steering toward that next mile marker on the horizon, when suddenly the road is overtaken by monsters. Let's call these devils "negative self-talk" and "feelings of fear, unworthiness, inadequacy, anxiety, depression, or shame." They're all throwing themselves at the windshield and banging the sides of the bus. The highway is so thick with these buggers that you can't possibly move forward. You could retreat, but that sucks, because now you're not following your compass. But even though you want to move forward, there is literally no way past these monsters. So what do you do?

You take a deep breath. You stop the bus. You open the door and you invite them on for the ride. You thank these troublemakers for trying to protect you; after all they *are* family. They're the offspring of your primitive survival instincts and your wounded inner child. They sound like that overprotective grandmother who adorned you with elbow and knee pads, a helmet, and bubble wrap just to go play on the park swings. If you tilt your head and squint, one of them bears a striking resemblance to your uncle Rex, who never made it as an artist and told you to stop wasting your time and get a "real" job. As they enter the bus, you politely redirect them when they try to grab the wheel or crank the radio to drown out your rational voice. You tell them to take a seat, explain that you're at the wheel and you're a capable driver. Now the road is clear and you can put the bus back in drive. You check your rearview mirror every once in a while to acknowledge your passengers, but your eyes are mainly fixed on the road ahead.

Another strategy for overcoming emotional and cognitive barriers is Tara Brach's RAIN technique, which she expertly outlines in her book *Radical Compassion*. RAIN stands for recognize, allow, investigate, and nurture.[2] Here's an example of how I use this technique when I feel anxiety. I pause and *recognize*,

"I'm feeling anxious." Next I *accept* it. I nonjudgmentally say, "Yep, here you are, anxiety. I see you." Then I *investigate* what is actually happening in my body: My teeth are clenched. My chest feels tight. I'm taking shallow breaths.

Ironically, just by noticing these things, some of them start to dissipate. I can consciously inhale deeply, roll my shoulders loose, and relax my jaw. But the last step is Brach's genius move: *nurture.* I conjure the sensation of someone coming to comfort me. For you, this could be a beloved family member, teacher, or maybe a sweet old dog that lays her head on your lap. For me, it's my dear friend, fellow musician, and amazing massage therapist, Jim. He burns sage at the end of every bodywork session and gently places his hands on certain points on my body with a silent prayer for serenity. I picture myself here with all my senses, and it helps the anxiety lessen. It takes all of twenty seconds to do, and I repeat as necessary.

The "Monsters on the Bus" and "RAIN" techniques stop destructive patterns of heaping negative emotions on yourself for feeling negative emotions. Can you see the irony in being angry at yourself for feeling anger? Or feeling anxious about feeling anxious? If you name the hard feelings and identify the negative thoughts, you can take a step back and realize you are not your thoughts and feelings. You are something deeper than that. You're the immutable core who is, in essence, perfect. These thoughts and feelings are impermanent. They will rise and fall. When I create this distance between thoughts/emotions and my true self, I am reminded that I have lived through hard times, and I can do it again. When I pair these techniques with identification of behavioral barriers, it helps me figure out my next steps and set realistic goals that get me moving in alignment with my compass.

There's a difference between retreating and failing forward. Failing forward might leave you with scrapes and bruises, but you're kinda proud of them, right? Like, "Hey, check out this cool bruise I got when I forgot all the lyrics to my song last night at that open mic. I totally fell on my face! It's alright, though. It'll heal and I'll bring a cheat sheet next time." Retreating, on the other hand, is never stepping on stage in the first place because you turned the bus around at the first sight of a monster. It leaves you feeling empty, listless, directionless. That is what happens when we abandon our purpose. McKay, Forsyth, and Eifert summarize beautifully the process and power of accepting our emotions: *"You're learning that your emotions aren't enemies and that you can have them just as they are, even the painful ones. And you're doing this for a purpose. This isn't just about feeling bad or being comfortable. It's about finding a way to feel what you feel and think what you think and do what matters to you."*[3]

Once more reality check: we need to differentiate between *abandoning* our creative self-growth and *temporarily* putting the bus in park because something else we value in life is crying out for our attention. Self-compassion is critical when you're in the midst of a major life change or crisis. I've had times in my life when I paused my creative pursuits, but I never doubted I would return to them because I knew creativity was part of my core.

So let's openly face our barriers. Yes, they may cause pain; pain is a part of life. It's not easy to welcome it, but it's far more productive than pushing it away, trying to outrun it, or retreating. And, oh boy, is it ever good songwriting material.

Playing Nicely with Others

Identifying and working with our barriers requires continuous self exploration. As we face challenges, it can also be helpful to join hands with others along the way. Art builds connections, so living as a thriving songwriter means becoming part of a creative community. Playing nicely with others requires taking a look inward while simultaneously opening to the world. The "others" you encounter on your purpose-driven journey come in the form of mentors, supporters, and collaborators. These categories aren't mutually exclusive; I've had mentors serve as both collaborators and supporters on my journey. Let's explore what each brings.

Mentors

There are the obvious mentors in our lives with titles like "expert" or "elder," but in reality, teachers are everywhere. The Buddhist concept of "beginner's mind" encourages us to view the world through fresh eyes every day. My son loves playing music for me on long car rides. He recently introduced me to phonk music. It's a subgenre of hip-hop that features unintelligible words, which freaked me out at first, but the more I listened, the more I realized that there was still an emotional message in the music. That's a valuable lesson for a word nerd like me. I've seen countless Ladies Rock Campers enroll in camp after watching their child perform at the Girls Rock Camp showcase. Watching their kid made them see their own need to connect with music. Artists in other disciplines can serve as mentors as well. Listening to podcasts or reading about techniques others use for choreography, painting, or costume design can be enlightening. The list of teachers is endless, so open your beginner's mind and seek mentors everywhere.

Supporters

It's lovely when we have cheerleaders around us, but sometimes we have to seek them out or tell people near and dear to us exactly what we need from them. Some people quite naturally cheer wildly at the end of our performances. (I'd love to have a million of these folks at every one of my shows.) But those closest to you might need to hear you say, "Hey, I'm doing this hard and brave thing and I'd appreciate your support. Can I count on you?" It's not realistic or fair to think everyone in your circle will understand your passion for songwriting, though. Folks on a similar journey could serve as a like-minded source of encouragement. If they hold a compass pointing in a similar direction, they understand your drive. A thriving songwriter needs a support network, so look for yours.

Collaborators

Collaborators, while essential, might be the trickiest group, because co-creating requires compromise and mental flexibility. At Girls and Ladies Rock Camp, we teach the "yes-and" approach employed by improv comedians. With this technique, you build on each other's ideas instead of dissing your partners' creative efforts and shutting down the scene before it unfolds. Opening your mind to the ideas of others requires a dose of humility, but allows you to create something you would never have created alone. Sometimes we need to let go of tightly held preferences and try something new. If you've got a killer lyric for a song, but it's not flowing in your co-written tune, learn to let go. You can always use it for a different song. With some collaborators, it's clear that you're on the same page, but it can't hurt to define a collective mission statement from the outset. I did this with my dear friends and bandmates in Gin, Chocolate & Bottle Rockets. Our mission statement has guided us since 2014 and it's made it possible for us to keep things in perspective during hard times and remember we have a shared purpose.

When working with others, it's easy to fall into the trap of comparison and competition. Jealousy is one of those sticky emotions we need to explore, so it doesn't become a barrier between you and your creative community. Instead of casting shadows on those we envy, how can we learn from them? Maybe this emotional barrier can help us identify areas for growth. Find friends who push you gently out of your protective bubble. When you become part of a healthy network, everyone spirals upward together.

Celebrating Successes

I'm a firm believer in creating opportunities to pause and acknowledge that you just passed another mile marker on your creative journey. Art teachers host gallery nights. Music and dance instructors schedule performances for students to show the results of their hard work to friends, family, and fellow students. In the absence of a mentor scheduling these events for you, you can get creative and find your own moments of revelry. You don't have to bust out the champagne and decorate the house, but please do if you desire! There are so many ways to pay tribute to a mission accomplished. Now that I'm decades into my music career, I love scheduling big events like album release parties, but I started with much smaller gestures. I used to write songs for my coworkers and schedule time with them to stay late after work. I'd sneak my guitar into the staff office and sing to them at the end of the day after everyone else had left. Having little dates like this encouraged me to polish my tunes and present them as gifts. These one-on-one "release parties" were still meaningful because I was acting in alignment with my purpose.

I am surrounded by friends who are taking inspiring first steps on their thriving songwriter journeys. Here are some of the ways they've recently celebrated:

- Megan recorded one of her first completed songs using Garageband. She combined the audio with a simple lyric video and posted it to her Facebook page.
- Carrie, a talented poet who is a relatively new guitarist/

singer/songwriter, scheduled a time to connect with Jenny, a fellow Ladies Rock Camper who is learning the bass. They just had a jam session together.

- Cathy worked with a group of friends to bring a performance to her mother's nursing home, so she could sing with a group of musicians with whom she had just begun collaborating.
- Jenn worked up the courage to email me a simple recording she made on her phone of the first song she wrote with both music and lyrics.
- Ellen just wrote her first three songs and is coming to my studio to record them with Jenna, a beloved mutual friend, studio musician, and Ladies Rock Camp instructor.

Speaking of accomplishing goals, it is time for us to celebrate reaching the final paragraph in this book. I've heard it said that you don't have to be able to slam dunk to be a good basketball coach. While I've not yet hit the charts with a song, I hope that I've helped you find your North Star and put wind in your sails for the voyage. Thank you for having the courage to board the ship. The ripples you create in the water impact the world.

Chapter 12: The Thriving Songwriter
Too Long, Didn't Read (TLDR) Summary

Aligning the value of creative self-expression with your strengths as a songwriter can impact the lives of others through connection and healing. With this in mind, you can write a songwriter's purpose statement to guide you like a compass on your creative journey. Simply having a compass will not clear the path of obstacles or put gas in the tank. Overcoming behavioral, emotional, and cognitive barriers is a necessary, and sometimes painful, part of the voyage. Numbing out or retreating from obstacles that stand between us and our goals leaves us feeling empty, whereas working through the discomfort of our barriers gives us a sense of accomplishment. To generate forward momentum, you can set goals, join forces with mentors/supporters/collaborators, and celebrate your successes.

Chapter 12: The Thriving Songwriter

1. Identify 3-5 behavioral, emotional, or cognitive barriers and write down one small step you could take toward moving past each barrier.
2. List the "monsters" you need to invite on your "bus."
3. Create an opportunity for yourself to celebrate the success of a finished song.
4. Revisit the mission statement you started in chapter 4, or write a mission statement for your authentic songwriter. Schedule reminders for yourself in your calendar to revisit this quarterly.

APPENDIX A: Lyric Chord Sheet Examples

<u>CENTER OF A STORM</u>

Beth Kille/Erik Kjelland (c) 2021

<u>INTRO</u>

Am

<u>CHORUS</u>

   Am   G

How would it feel? What would it be like

   Am G   F

Falling asleep in the center of a storm

    Am   G

Floating in peace, covered in starlight

    Am G F

How can I turn my chaos into calm

      Am

In the center of a storm

<u>VERSE 1</u>

G   Dm   F   C   G

With my eyes wide open, I lay here hoping for a swift reprieve

G   Dm   F   C   G

From the thundering soldiers with guns to their shoulders all pointed at me

    Am G   Am   G

I just need a little sleep. Something to pacify me

APPENDIX A: Lyric Chord Sheet Examples

CHORUS

        Am   **G**

How would it feel? What would it be like

        Am   **G**   **F**

Falling asleep in the center of a storm

          Am   **G**

Floating in peace, covered in starlight

        Am   **G**   **F**

How can I turn my chaos into calm

            Am

In the center of a storm

VERSE 2

G   Dm   F   C   G

I feel the fingers of lightning, the grip is tightening around my skin

G   Dm   F   C   G

The current invades me, my reverie wasted in the howling wind

          Am   G   Am   G

I just need a little sleep, a beautiful dream

BRIDGE

          F   G

The violence and the rain, Circle round the drain

         C   Am

With carnage and pain, spilling from my veins

       F   G   Am   G

Something surreal, how would it feel, oh how would it feel

APPENDIX A: Lyric Chord Sheet Examples

<u>CHORUS</u>

    Am   G

How would it feel? What would it be like

    Am   G   F

Falling asleep in the center of a storm

      Am   G

Floating in peace, covered in starlight

     Am   G   F

How can I turn my chaos into peace

    Am   G

How would it feel? What would it be like

    Am   G   F

Falling asleep in the center of a storm

      Am   G

Floating in peace, covered in starlight

     Am   G   F

How can I turn my chaos into calm

<u>OUTRO</u>

Am G F repeated

APPENDIX A: Lyric Chord Sheet Examples

WILD HORSES B Kille ©2022

INTRO: F G Em Am // F G Am Am

VERSE 1

F   G   Em   Am

I rode in upon this horse but forgot to take the reins

F   G   Am   Am

Barely holding on in rough terrain

F   G   Em   Am

Believing stories. Forgetting to get to truth

F   G   Am   Am

it's driving this divide between me and you

CHORUS

C   F   Am   G

I'm gonna look in the mirror instead of staring out the window

   C   F   Am   G

Gonna study every line upon my face

C   F   Am   G

Now I'm riding straight into the thunder and lightning

      F   C   G   G

'Cause I know can't grow without the rain

    F G Em Am // F G Am Am

without the rain

APPENDIX A: Lyric Chord Sheet Examples

<u>**CHORUS**</u>

       Am   G

How would it feel? What would it be like

       Am   G   F

Falling asleep in the center of a storm

        Am   G

Floating in peace, covered in starlight

        Am   G   F

How can I turn my chaos into peace

        Am   G

How would it feel? What would it be like

       Am   G   F

Falling asleep in the center of a storm

        Am   G

Floating in peace, covered in starlight

       Am   G   F

How can I turn my chaos into calm

<u>**OUTRO**</u>

Am G F repeated

APPENDIX B: Noun, Adjective, Verb List

Nouns

Smile	Sky	Clouds	Dream	Heart	Eyes
Ears	Hair	Face	Head (any body part!	Love	Mind
Thoughts	Notions	Stars	Whispers	Mess	Day
Excuses	Pride	Hunger	Garden	Tree	Mountain
Car (brands)	Memory	Hole	Happiness	Sadness	Anger
Person	Girl/Woman	Boy/Man	Brother	Sister	Father
Mother	Child	Son	Daughter	Intentions	Judgment
Logic	Senses (sight, touch, etc.)	Feeling	Devil	Angel	God/gods
Church	Foods (bread, fruit, etc.)	Drinks	Ocean/Sea	River	Rock

Adjectives

Abandoned	Abusive	Abbreviated	Addictive	Aloof	Apathetic
Aromatic	Astonishing	Beautiful	Broken	Bashful	Blinding
Big-mouthed	Breezy	Ceaseless	Cheerful	Childlike	Chilly
Comfortable	Colors (any color)	Cowardly	Crazy	Crooked	Cynical
Damaged	Deafening	Devilish	Dirty	Deranged	Deserted
Disagreeable	Dizzy	Dramatic	Dazzling	Dysfunctional	Drunk/drunken
Dry	Deep/Deeply	Domineering	Eager	Edible	Empty
Erratic	Faded	Fancy	Fast	Faulty	Fearless
Fertile	Filthy	Flawless	Forgetful	Friendly	Frustrated
Flavors (cherry, chocolate, etc.)	Gaudy	Gentle	Glamorous	Graceful	Gaping

APPENDIX B: Noun, Adjective, Verb List

Gross	Groovy	Guilty	Greedy	Grumpy	Guarded
Happy	Heavenly	Harmonious	Hurried	Hungry	Hurt
Hysterical	Honorable	Idiotic	Jealous	Jaded	Jumbled
Kind hearted	Lopsided	Lacking	Lazy	Lying	Macho
Maddening	Magical	Melodic	Merciful	Mighty	Mundane
Naive	Needy	Nervous	Nostalgic	Nosy	Painful
Pathetic	Peaceful	Proud	Psychedelic	Sad	Silent
Shocking	Silky	Sweltering	Tangy	Tall	Tasty
Threatening	Twisted	Ugly	Uneven	Vast	Venomous
Victorious	Voiceless	Wounded			

Verbs

Accept	Accuse	Adapt	Adhere	Adjust	Admire
Admit	Adore	Advance	Aggravate	Aim	Antagonize
Apologize	Appear	Argue	Attach	Avoid	Awaken
Attack	Badmouth	Backtrack	Baffle	Bait	Balance
Bare	Bargain	Barge	Bark	Bawl	Beat
Beckon	Beg	Behave	Behold	Believe	Bet
Betray	Bicker	Bite	Blame	Bleed	Breathe
Break	Browse	Buckle	Bury	Calm	Caress
Carry	Catch	Cease	Chase	Coax	Collapse
Color	Complain	Control	Command	Commiserate	Confess
Crash	Creep	Cross	Crimp	Cringe	Cry
Criticize	Dance	Deal	Delare	Defend	Deflate
Defy	Demand	Dare	Draw	Dream	Drink
Echo	Explain	Face	Fabricate	Forget	Forgive

APPENDIX B: Noun, Adjective, Verb List

Fume	Gag	Gawk	Gaze	Grasp	Grieve
Growl	Handle	Heat	Fold	Howl	Hurt
Judge	Ignore	Imagine	Insult	Invited	Jump
Kick	Kiss	Land	Laugh	Leap	Lunge
March	Memorize	Misunderstand	Mock	Mourn	Nag
Obsess	Outwit	Panic	Philosophize	Punish	Question
Raise	Reel	Resist	Restrain	Search	Seek
Stare	Salute	Seep	Speculate	Squeal	Stifle
Suffer	Surrender	Swagger	Swim	Tackle	Taste
Tease	Tickle	Tremble	Turn	Uncoil	Unlock
Urge	Vow	Watch	Wait	Whisper	Wince
Wink	Wobble	Wrangle	Wrestle	Yawn	Yelp

http://www.esldesk.com/vocabulary/verbs/

APPENDIX C: Roman Numerals and Chord Function Chart in All Keys

Roman Numeral	I ("one")*	ii ("2 minor")	iii ("3 minor)	IV ("four")	V ("five")	vi ("6 minor")
Function	stable	transitional	stable	transitional	unstable	stable
	A	Bm	C#m	D	E	F#m
	Bb	Cm	Dm	Eb	F	Gm
	B	C#m	D#m	E	F#	G#m
	C	Dm	Em	F	G	Am
	C#	D#	Fm	F#	G#	A#m
*The key is always named after the I chord	D	Em	F#m	G	A	Bm
	Eb	Fm	Gm	Ab	Bb	Cm
	E	F#m	G#m	A	B	C#m
	F	Gm	Am	Bb	C	Dm
	F#	G#m	A#m	B	C#	D#m
	G	Am	Bm	C	D	Em
	Ab	Bb	Cm	Db	Eb	Fm

Note: this chart deliberately does not contain a seventh column with the diminished chord for simplicity since this is a less frequently-used chord.

ACKNOWLEDGEMENTS

It's been a joyful learning experience to write this book. There are many people who walked beside me on this journey that I have to thank.

Firstly, to my editor, Jenn Morea. You've read these pages countless times and I've never once felt your enthusiasm wane. This book would still be a bunch of half-finished chapters of bullet points and misspelled sentence fragments if you hadn't approached me at Ladies Rock Camp back in February of 2023 to tell me about your skills. You boosted my confidence and helped me turn my ramblings into a real book. And somewhere along the way you turned into a dear friend. I cannot thank you enough.

I also have immense gratitude for my personal Fab Four Dream Team: Jenn Morea, Carrie Schonhoff, Ellen Damschen, and Laura Lang. Thanks for all your time and brain power beta testing this book with me every Monday night for six weeks in the fall of 2023. Jenn, I already thanked you above, but I just wanted to acknowledge that you didn't have to sit through these meetings, and it was a source of great comfort and reassurance to me that you were willing to do it. Carrie, you offered so much insight and I was stoked by the way you took off and ran with the new knowledge you gleaned from the manuscript. Your poetic talents and soulfulness shone through in the beautiful songs you shared with us in those meetings. Laura, I can't believe my good fortune of having a kindhearted educator who doubles as a pro songwriter in my test group. Your feedback was thoughtful, thorough, supportive, and invaluable. And Ellen, you went above and beyond. Your fine-toothed comb read-through of the draft, especially of the music theory chapter, was beyond helpful. I also loved watching the floodgate open on your muse this past year. Your songs rock. I'm inspired by your focus, intelligence, generosity, and creativity.

I'm grateful for all my bandmates and co-writers over the years. Starting with Andy Ziehli and the Watershed crew, my Clear Blue Betty buds and the rotating cast of characters in the Sing It Sister House Band; you literally stood beside me as I grew into my skin as a performer and writer. Thanks for rocking out and putting up with me. We definitely had fun! To my first songwriting instructor, Eric Hester: thank you for the tools to begin this journey. You taught me so much. To my Texas mentor and co-writer, Connie Mims: your giving spirit inspired me in so many ways. I'm so lucky you took me under your wing during my year in Houston. To my dear friend and collaborator, Gene Reynolds: I loved our cowriting times together in Nashville and so admire your musical skills as well as your kind and gentle soul. To Jen Farley and Shawndell Marks, my cherished Gin, Chocolate & Bottle Rockets bandmates: you've cheered me on throughout this process. I love that I have my two besties as bandmates and we can celebrate together! Your heart-centered approach to life fills my soul. I love you both beyond measure. To my Beth Kille Band boys: you're amazing. Michael Tully, I know you'll never read this, but you're my favorite beast-mode guitarist. Michael Mood, I'm lucky to have a bassist beside me who also doubles as a force of creative talent. I appreciate your willingness to share your experience with writing and publishing too.

I was going to lump Erik Kjelland into the last paragraph

of bandmates and cowriters, but a man of this many talents warrants his own paragraph. Erik, not only are you a treasured collaborator, co-conspirator, and fellow ambidextrous, minivan-driving Pisces, but you're my go-to man for design work. I'm so grateful for your work ethic and trustworthiness. You helped make this book a physical reality.

I also want to recognize the Madison, Wisconsin area music community as a whole. There are so many incredibly talented and supportive people on this scene. The good folks of the Madison Area Music Association like Rick Tvedt, Roy Elkins, and Ty Christian, as well as figures like Karin Wolf of the Madison Arts Commission and Mark Fraire of Dane Arts are keeping the music alive and well in this "77 square miles surrounded by reality" and beyond. Music legends like Mike Massey, Mary Gaines, Chris Wagoner, and Mark Croft and producer/engineers like Jake Johnson and Audrey Martinovich are continual sources of goodness in the world. This music scene is sturdy upon the foundations you've all built.

I would be remiss if I didn't give a shoutout to all of my Girls and Ladies Rock Camp humans. To all my fellow staffers: your dedication to our organizational mission is causing a beautiful ripple effect of creative, accepting, positive world-changing strength and love. Go team! To every camper who has shown up to do the brave thing: I see you. Thank you for sharing your gifts with the world. And thank you for teaching me while I taught.

To Jackie Bradley, Mandi Viergutz, and John Gazeley (rest in peace): thank you for allowing me to share your stories on these pages. You inspired just by being your beautiful, vulnerable, honest selves.

To the fans who show up and cheer me on at shows: you are the reason I keep writing. I cherish the energetic loop that cycles from you to me and back to you when I'm on stage. This book wouldn't exist without all of you.

To my Mom, Sue De Kelver; my Dad, Bob De Kelver; and my sister, Amy De Kelver: growing up in a house surrounded by your love is a debt I can never repay. Mom, you will never fully comprehend how deeply your creative life has influenced me. You shared your voice and made me realize that I could share mine. Dad, you're my source of unconditional love and my all-time favorite hype-man. If I had sneezed on a piece of paper and called it art, you would've celebrated it. And Mom would've kindly encouraged me to reach a bit further. You are the perfect pair as parents. I won the mom-dad jackpot.

And last but not least, to my husband Tony Kille and my son Gus Kille: my life would be so dull without you two weirdos. I love you both with my whole heart. Gus, you make me laugh everyday. I love your imagination and the way you share your musings and experiences with me. I'm so proud of the thoughtful, hysterical, and clever young man you are. Tony, you are the drummer I hear in my head when I write and the heartbeat of my life. I can't believe how lucky I am to have met my soulmate at the age of nineteen. It was so convenient that my soulmate was willing to learn to play a drum kit while I learned to write, play guitar, and sing. (I still secretly think it was all motivated by your desire to stare at my butt on stage.) Thanks for your trust and partnership. We've made a lot of this life together, including a lot of music. I am so thankful for that.

NOTES

CHAPTER 1: WHY PEOPLE LISTEN TO MUSIC

I. I originally encountered this quote on Tara Brach's website. Tara Brach, "Awakening From the Trance of Unworthiness," *Inquiring Mind* 17, no. 2 (Spring 2001), https://inquiringmind.com/article/1702_20_brach_awakening-from-unworthiness/.

2. Robert Jourdain, *Music, the Brain, and Ecstasy: How Music Captures Our Imagination.* (New York: Harper Perennial, 1997), 163.

3. For a more comprehensive understanding of vulnerability, read Brené Brown's *Daring Greatly: How the Courage to Be Vulnerable Transforms the Way We Live, Love, Parent, and Lead.* Brené Brown, "The Power of Vulnerability," TEDxHouston, streamed live on November 22, 2023, YouTube video, 00:05:26, https://www.youtube.com/watch?v=X4Qm9cGRub0.

CHAPTER 2: WHY YOUR BODY, MIND, AND SPIRIT MATTER

I. James Collins, *Good to Great: Why Some Companies Make the Leap and Others Don't.* (New York: Harper Business, 2001).

CHAPTER 4: WHY DO YOU WANT TO WRITE SONGS?

I. Christine Whelan, PhD, *The Big Picture: A Guide to Finding Your Purpose in Life* (West Conshohocken: Templeton Press, 2016).

CHAPTER 12: THE THRIVING SONGWRITER

I. Matthew McKay, John P. Forsyth and Georg H. Eifert, *Your Life on Purpose: How to Find What Matters & Create the Life You Want* (Oakland: New Harbinger Publications, 2010).

2. For more information about RAIN, you may enjoy exploring the resources on Tara Brach's website. Tara Brach, *Radical Compassion: Learning to Love Yourself and Your World with the Practice of RAIN* (New York: Viking, 2019).

3. McKay, Forsyth and Eifert, *Your Life on Purpose,* 159.